DREAM LIKE A CHAMPION

DREAM LIKE

 The publisher gratefully acknowledges *Hail Varsity* magazine's assistance in the preparation of this book.

A CHAMPION

*Wins, Losses, and Leadership
the Nebraska Volleyball Way*

John Cook *with* Brandon Vogel

University of Nebraska Press | Lincoln and London

Library of Congress Control Number: 2017943808

Set in Lyon Text by John Klopping.

To Mom and Dad, who never let me quit
and taught me to work hard for everything.

To Wendy, the ultimate coach's wife:
understanding of the demands coaches
face and the sacrifices they make, willing
to make many sacrifices of her own, and
always there for all Huskers.

To Lauren and Taylor, who have had to
share their dad with volleyball teams
and have inspired their parents with their
hard work and dedication.

To Tom Osborne, the consummate coach,
mentor, and role model.

CONTENTS

PHOTOGRAPHS

PREFACE

A text message arrives at 2:16 a.m., the glow from my phone lighting the darkened hotel room. As a coach I am used to sleepless nights, particularly before the biggest games—and they do not come any bigger than an NCAA Championship match. It was December 16, 2006.

In less than seventeen hours we would face Stanford in Omaha for the national title. It was Stanford's twelfth appearance in the national-title match and the Cardinal had already won six national championships, the most in college volleyball at the time. This stage was far from foreign to them.

When the preseason poll came out that season, Nebraska was number one and Stanford was number four, but the Cardinal received only one fewer first-place vote than we did. By the time the seeds were announced for the NCAA Tournament at the end of the season, we were 27-1 and champions of the Big 12 Conference, and we had done enough to earn the top seed. Stanford finished the regular season 25-3, won the Pac-10 Conference title, and earned the second seed in the tournament. It would be just the second time in the history of the tournament that the top two seeds faced off in the final game.

To the outside observer it may have looked like everything was going according to plan. Here were the two best teams in the country playing for the national title. Volleyball insiders, however, knew that a Pac-10 team had won the previous five national titles. Many of the real die-hard volleyball people inside the sport thought Stanford had the best team.

There were plenty of reasons to think that and plenty of players on that team to keep an opposing coach awake at night. A pair of sophomores, outside hitter Cynthia Barboza and middle blocker Foluke Akinradewo, led Stanford. Both were selected as First Team All-Americans by the American Volleyball Coaches Association, and each would earn the honor two more times in college before going on to careers with the U.S. National Team. Stanford junior setter Bryn Kehoe was a Second Team All-American. Senior outside hitter Kristin Richards was a Third Team All-American.

We countered with four All-Americans of our own: freshman setter Rachel Holloway, sophomore outside hitter Jordan Larson, junior right side hitter Sarah Pavan, and junior middle blocker Tracy Stalls. If people were thinking Stanford was the best team in college volleyball, I was fine letting my team think the same.

The day before the match I sent one of our student managers all over Omaha searching for a DVD copy of *Do You Believe in Miracles*, a documentary on the 1980 U.S. Olympic hockey team. That team, made up of amateur and collegiate players, famously knocked off a much more experienced Soviet Union team in what *Sports Illustrated* named the "Top Sports Moment of the Twentieth Century." The team needed to see that film.

We eventually found a copy at a nearby bookstore. I had our video staff add some of our season highlights to the end of the film and we screened it for the team. Afterward we talked about the level of belief that that U.S. team had to have had to think it could beat a Soviet hockey program that had won the previous four gold medals and 27 of its previous 29 games in Olympic play over two decades. That was the example we left our players with as they headed off to bed.

A few hours later, shortly after 2:00 in the morning, the text message arrived: "Dream big. Dream like a champion tonight."

The text went out to the whole team and it didn't come from a captain or one of our four All-Americans. It came from senior Dani Mancuso, a reserve outside hitter from Omaha. She was preparing to play her final match as a Husker.

In high school Dani had been one of the best prep players in the country. I first saw her play at a club tournament and she blew me away. "Holy cow," I thought the first time I watched her warm up. She was an explosive player.

Dani went on to set two Nebraska Class B state records for kills when playing for Omaha Gross High School, and we had to out-recruit a handful of schools, including Stanford, to get her. She started fifteen matches for us as a freshman in 2003, but her performance was somewhat erratic. She had what I thought was a breakout performance against Notre Dame as a sophomore in 2004. We were down 2 sets to 1 in a match against the Fighting Irish and Dani came off the bench to record 10 kills over the final 2 sets, powering us to the win. I gave her a chance to start after that, but she struggled in a few games and was back on the bench a couple of games later.

About a month after that, Dani showed her potential again with 22 kills and .559 hitting on the road against Kansas State, but it turned out to be another flash-in-the-pan type of performance. As her career progressed, her number of starts decreased, from fifteen that first season to nine starts as sophomore and only five starts over her junior and senior seasons combined.

Before her senior season started, Dani asked me what she would need to do to be a starter. "Well, first of all, you need to touch over ten feet," I said. "That would be a start." Dani was physically gifted coming out of high school, but I was not convinced she had worked very hard at Nebraska, so I was trying to spur her along. When she touched ten feet that summer—ten-feet-two-inches, is what I recall— she raced over to tell me.

It was clear to me then how badly Dani wanted to play, but her biggest hurdle was simply our roster in 2006. At outside hitter we had Christina Houghtelling, the 2005 national player of the year, and Jordan Larson, a future Olympian. Sarah Pavan, another future Olympian, was on the right side. That would have been a tough rotation for anyone to crack, but on our team trip to China that summer Christina hurt her shoulder and was out for the season. That left Dani as our only backup hitter and she ended up playing in every match in 2006.

Dani was definitely a good player, but on this team—which, in addition to all of the All-Americans, featured one of my future assistant coaches, Dani Busboom—she was the weak link in our regular rotation. The other girls had played plenty of tough points in the big matches. Dani did not have that type of experience. If we would get to a defining moment against Stanford, she was the one I was worried about. And that is why her text message meant something.

The impossible task facing coaches is to remove as much uncertainty as possible from games that can be pretty random. You train athletes to help them reach the peak of their abilities, you practice plays thousands of times so they become second nature, you look for new ways to motivate and give your team mental strength, all in the hope of knowing that when the pivotal play needs to be made, it will be made.

But you can never really know. At the highest level, 1 or 2 points—a random bounce, a lucky dig—can often decide the game. You do all the work to get as close as you can to certainty, all while knowing you will never quite get there. Dani's text was as close as you get.

When I looked at my phone that night, I took a deep breath and thought, "Okay, we've got a shot." If Dani was feeling confident enough to send that text to our entire team, I knew our team as a whole had to have been feeling pretty good about that night's match.

We played it in front of 17,209 fans that Saturday in Omaha, at the time the largest crowd ever for a U.S. college volleyball match. Stanford took the first game, but we won the next three. They were all tight games, championship-level volleyball, but we had the extra edge. We were a team that had total commitment from each and every player.

That is the level I am always trying to reach as a coach. That is when you know that the foundation you have laid is as strong as it can possibly be. That is when I can relax, at least a little bit, and just go out and coach. That is when dreaming big goes from being a goal to being an entire philosophy. It is the one that has defined my career as a coach.

DREAM LIKE A CHAMPION

1

Learning to Lead

"The game is over-coached and under-taught."
—PETE NEWELL, Hall of Fame basketball coach

I always knew I wanted to help mentor and lead young people, but I never planned for it to be as a volleyball coach. That was more the result of timing and circumstance. Life has a way of rewarding you if you are receptive to the opportunities it presents. Especially if they are not the opportunities you are necessarily expecting.

When I first became a volleyball coach in 1982, I had to go to the library and look for a book on the sport just to understand the indoor game. By then I was a football coach who had played a few summers of beach volleyball, and a football coach is what I thought I would continue to be. The football mentality meshed well with my upbringing.

I grew up south of San Diego in Chula Vista, California. My mother, Bobby Jo, had me when she was seventeen years old and still a junior in high school. My father, Chris, was eighteen and a senior. We lived on a nine-acre lemon ranch.

It was a five-acre lemon ranch when my great-grandparents, Maxwell and Hazel Goes Cook, homesteaded there in 1911. My great-grandmother was an amazing woman; she graduated from Smith College in Northampton, Massachusetts, in 1906, just twenty-one years after it had opened. Most men did not have the opportunity to attend college in those years, much less women.

After getting married, Maxwell and Hazel were living in Chicago when Maxwell contracted scarlet fever. There were no antibiotics then, so a doctor told them the best treatment would be to move to a place with better air quality. Many places would have offered better air than the stockyard stench of Chicago, but they picked the place that was perhaps the total opposite: San Diego. They purchased five acres at $25.00 per acre and built a house overlooking the ocean.

Chula Vista had just been incorporated as a town then, but it was already known as the "Lemon Capital of the World." My grandparents started planting lemon trees and adding acres; in the years to come the ranch grew to include fifty-five acres and more than fourteen hundred lemon trees. Hazel became a community leader almost immediately. She is credited with helping create school lunch programs in California. During the Great Depression many families struggled to have enough food, so my great-grandmother and her friends would make soup, load it into a Ford Model A, and drive it to nearby schools. She went on to serve on the school board for fifty years, eventually retiring at age eighty-seven. There is an elementary school named after her in Chula Vista.

Hazel also earned a spot on the all-male board of directors at one of the nearby citrus packinghouses and loved to exercise. She built a tennis court on her property and played every day. When her doctor told her she had to give up tennis at age seventy, she replaced the tennis court with a swimming pool and swam every day. That exercise helped offset a couple of her vices. I remember she smoked two packs a day and every night at 6:00 p.m. she had a martini. At 6:15 p.m. she had another martini.

Hazel was never afraid to make her own way. She was the backbone of our family and I spent a lot of time with her while growing up. She was a great mentor for so many kids in the area over the course of her life, including me.

When lemon ranching hit an economic downturn in the 1960s, Hazel sold off most of her land to Rohr Inc., an aerospace manufacturing company, which built its factory in Chula Vista and needed housing for its employees. But there was still enough land left for my parents to have a house. My dad grew lemons and cucumbers on the land and picked up work as a welder for Rohr to make ends meet.

I started selling cucumbers by the side of the road when I was old enough to work. If I wanted money to buy something I had to save the money, so I picked up whatever additional jobs I could. I mowed lawns, detailed cars, did cleanup jobs, whatever it took. It was very much a working-class existence for my family, but my dad was always a people person and that was a trait that would eventually help me land my first coaching job.

I was the first member of my family to go to college. I attended the University of San Diego on a basketball scholarship. Before my senior season, USD transitioned from Division II to Division I in basketball and my coach, Jim Brovelli, a basketball lifer who went on to be an NBA scout and assistant coach for a handful of teams, told me what I already knew as a six-foot-three forward: "You know, John, I don't think you're going to play much." That was the end of my basketball career, but it would lead to the start of a career in coaching.

In the summer of 1979 my younger brother, Dave, and I moved into an apartment overlooking South Mission Beach. We lived there with Hank and John Ashworth, brothers who went on to found the golf-apparel company Ashworth. An apartment on the beach was a pretty good arrangement for four college guys, all of us athletes.

We watched from our apartment window as the same group of middle-aged guys headed down to the beach each day to play volleyball. "Looks fun," one of us said, and finally one day we went down there and asked them to teach us how to play.

As basketball players, we were athletic enough to pick up the sport quickly, but the beach veterans—teachers and physical education instructors from the nearby schools, for the most part—knew the ins and outs of the game. I do not think we won a game that first summer, but we were hooked on beach volleyball.

I did not like losing much, so, without really knowing it at the time, I started coaching. Similar to classic pickup basketball rules, the rules of the beach were that you had to win to stay on the court. Lose and you might not get back on. We had to get better if we wanted to keep playing. I started setting up drills for us to do. It was simple stuff but always with a clear goal in mind. We would draw a circle in the sand and try to pass the ball into the circle. We had to get ten in a row before we could quit. Then we would toss and hit ten balls as far as we could down the beach, chasing each one in the soft sand for conditioning. We slowly started getting better.

Later that summer I landed my first coaching job. My dad had started working as a team representative for a local sporting goods company. He was the guy all the local teams—San Diego State, USD, the Padres, the Chargers, the Clippers before they moved to Los Angeles—called when they needed equipment or uniforms. He was also supplying most of the high schools in San Diego and he had the right personality for the job. Through his network of connections my dad heard that Coronado High School was looking for an assistant football coach. I had played football in high school, quarterback and linebacker, and got the job. That fall I was coaching the defensive line and linebackers, completing my undergraduate degree at USD, stealing away to the beach when I could to play volleyball, and generally loving life.

After my first season at Coronado and once I was done with school, the Ashworth brothers, Dave, and I were ready to get back to the beach for another summer of volleyball.

The drills had paid off. Not only were we starting to win some games and staying on the court, we had started to win enough to enter some tournaments. Over the next couple of years Dave and I played enough beach volleyball to work our way up the rankings in the just-formed Association of Volleyball Professionals tour. In those tournaments we faced beach legends like Karch Kiraly, Sinjin Smith, and Randy Stoklos. We also occasionally ran up against legends of a different kind, too. I played against Bill Walton and Wilt Chamberlain a couple of times, two seven-foot basketball hall of famers who fell in love with volleyball after their professional playing careers were over.

I, too, was falling deeper in love with the sport in that summer of 1980, but I also fell in love with a volleyball player who I eventually married. I met Wendy at a beach tournament while she was still a member of San Diego State's indoor team. I did not know it at the time, but watching Wendy play for the Aztecs, where she would earn All-America honors twice, would be the only experience I would have with the indoor game when I needed it a few years later.

But there was more football to coach before that. In 1980, my second year at Coronado, our defensive coordinator came down with mononucleosis during the first week of practice and I was suddenly running the defense. We played in the city league, which was a really tough league, particularly for a second-year coach just out of college.

We ended up winning our conference title in 1980 and had the top-ranked defense in the league. In the California Interscholastic Federation playoffs we faced San Diego's Abraham Lincoln High School. Lincoln was led by future Heisman Trophy winner Marcus Allen, and he was catching passes from his younger brother, Damon, who went on to become one of the greatest quarterbacks in the history of the Canadian Football League. The Allen brothers, not surprisingly, ended our playoff run.

I knew I wanted to be a football coach at that point, but I wasn't going to get by on the $1,000 a season Coronado could offer an assistant coach who was not also teaching. I wanted to teach, but finding a job proved more difficult than I expected.

In 1981 I took the defensive coordinator job at the University of San Diego High School with the promise that I would get a teaching job the following year. When that teaching job never materialized, I was suddenly in a tough spot. Wendy and I were getting married and I had a job I loved but a salary that certainly was not paying the bills.

A few weeks before the 1982 football season started, Francis Parker School, a private school just up the street from USD, called to offer me a teaching position. It came with a $10,000 contract and an apartment. The only catch was no more football.

Instead, I was asked to coach girls' volleyball, girls' basketball, middle school boys' basketball, and middle school boys' track. I loved being a football coach more than just about anything, but with this new job I had health insurance and a place to live, so it was not a hard decision to make. I became a volleyball coach and the extent of my experience with the indoor game was what I had been able to pick up watching Wendy play the previous fall and what I could cram from an impromptu crash course. In the few weeks before the season started, I went to a couple of nearby clinics and practices to learn what I could and picked up a book to help me understand the rules. Away we went.

Girls' athletics were a fairly new thing in that era. Many of the girls on that first team were competing and training for the first time. There wasn't much of a foundation there compared to what a coach would have now, so I coached them just like I had my high school football players. We went on five-mile soft-sand runs on South Mission Beach and I gave them goals to hit. "If you can't make it back in this amount of time, you're not going to play," I told them.

Maybe I did not know how to do it any other way at that point in my brief coaching career, but it worked. The girls that stuck it out became a mentally tough and in-shape team. We became the first San Diego school to make it to the state playoff in girls' volleyball, a sport then dominated by schools in Los Angeles, San Francisco, and Sacramento.

In 1985 Francis Parker made it all the way to the state semifinals in the small schools division. There we faced a Southern California Christian High School team that was led by setter Cinnamon Williams, who went on to play at UCLA, and outside hitter Tara Cross, who played in four Olympic Games on the U.S. Women's National Team. That was a tough tandem to handle and we got swept 15–9, 15–1, 15–7. A year later, however, we won our first state title and then did it again in 1987 while stringing together a 90-match winning streak. I was perfectly content. The football coach had become a volleyball coach.

While I was happily coaching volleyball, however, Wendy was killing herself working sixty- or seventy-hour weeks at Price Waterhouse. It was time to take the next step up the coaching ladder.

In San Diego in 1986 there was no such thing as club volleyball. One night over beers and tacos a friend of mine, Dick Templeman, and I decided to change that. We founded the San Diego Volleyball Club and had two hundred boys and girls come out that year. San Diego offered the one thing most fledgling athletic programs in any sport need: talent. There were a lot of good volleyball players around the area and they needed a place to play outside of their school teams. We offered them that place.

By 1988 our top club team had ten players who would go on to sign with Division I programs. Not just any programs, but powerhouses like UCLA, Hawaii, and USC, among others. These were the real heavyweights of the sport at the time. When you have that much talent in one place, the college coaches cannot help but find you. That is how Terry Pettit found me.

Pettit, a published poet with a master of fine arts degree in creative writing, was Nebraska's second volleyball coach after taking over the program in 1977. Before Pettit, Pat Sullivan had guided Nebraska through its first two years of intercollegiate play with an 83-21 record. Pettit was an instant success, winning both the Big 8 Conference regular-season and tournament titles in each of his first nine seasons. In 1986 Pettit led the Cornhuskers to the NCAA championship game, making Nebraska the first school from outside California or Hawaii to ever play for a national title in women's volleyball.

In those years Pettit would bring his Nebraska team to San Diego every spring. He was a friend of Doug Dannevic, then the head women's volleyball coach at the University of California–San Diego. Those annual trips offered Nebraska the chance to scrimmage against Dannevic's team. It also gave Pettit the chance to mix in some golf while doing a little recruiting.

My top San Diego Volleyball Club team at that time was good enough to scrimmage Pettit's Nebraska squad, which was coming off a regional appearance in the NCAA tournament. After the scrimmage Pettit asked me out to lunch and we picked each other's brains for a while. It was a pleasant but perfectly normal conversation between two volleyball coaches.

Or so I thought. It turned into much more a few months later. In June of 1988 Pettit got me on the phone. "We have a position open," he said. "Would you be interested?" I was interested.

Nebraska flew me out for an interview. It was maybe my second or third time on a plane. I got to Lincoln and they put me up at the Cornhusker Hotel, an opulent local landmark in the heart of downtown. For a teacher and coach whose vacations consisted of taking his wife hiking and then sleeping in the truck, showing up to a fancy hotel and having a gift bag waiting felt like the big time.

I did not have to think too hard about taking that job either. Next stop: Nebraska.

We pulled into Ogallala, Nebraska, on August 5, 1988. We had been towing a rented trailer full of all our belongings behind our Toyota pickup truck for thirteen hundred miles. It was a 105-degree day and the nearby feedlot smelled like feedlots tend to smell in 105-degree heat. We got to our motel room, opened the door, flipped on the light, and watched as cockroaches scattered.

This was Wendy's introduction to our new home state. She started sobbing. "Where are you taking me?" she asked. "If this is Nebraska, we're out of here."

"No, Lincoln is a little different," I said.

And it was different. For me it was a little bit of a dream destination. Not only was I joining a volleyball program that was serving notice that the sport could flourish at the college level outside of California, but I was also going to have the opportunity to study Nebraska's powerful football program up close.

Like all sports fans at the time, I had watched those classic Nebraska-Oklahoma football games on Thanksgiving Day. I loved the option offense. I admired coach Tom Osborne, or "Dr. Tom," as he was sometimes referred to by television broadcasters. "Why is a doctor coaching football?" I recall asking my parents as a kid while we watched the Cornhuskers battle the Sooners one year. "Does he take care of the players?" He was not a medical doctor, of course. Osborne had a doctorate in educational psychology.

I was working on my own postgraduate degree through San Diego State University at the time. It took me seven years to finish my course work as I worked on it in the summers between coaching duties. It was a job on top of a job, but it was time well spent because it provided the chance to study under Dr. Brent Rushall, a professor at San

Diego State who was doing some groundbreaking work in the field of coaching theory.

Rushall, a native of Australia, made his name working with Olympic swimmers. He is the author of numerous books and scholarly articles in a field that was just starting to develop in the mid-1980s. Today we would call it sports psychology. When I completed my degree in 1991, a short, punchy name for it didn't yet exist, so technically my master's degree is in teaching and coaching effectiveness.

Looking back on my years as an assistant at Nebraska, I spent three seasons learning to coach at the college level while absorbing wisdom from a one-of-a-kind group of thinkers. I had one of the foremost authorities in sports psychology guiding my graduate work. I was an assistant to one of the most cerebral and cutting-edge coaches in the sport of volleyball. When I wanted to absorb even more I could pop over to football practice and watch how one of the best coaches in college football operated one of the best programs in the country. I was very lucky.

In addition to the mental side of coaching and leadership, I was also getting an advanced course in running a program. I was not just an assistant coach at Nebraska in those years. I also served as our recruiting coordinator, strength and conditioning coach, the team's direct connection to the academic advising center—three major components of any successful college program.

Pettit taught me a lot about setting up a practice plan. He was an Apple computer groupie long before most anyone else. There could not have been many other volleyball programs using computers the way we did back then. Pettit's Macs were always running, spitting out new diagrams and practice plans, contributing to the already unbearable heat in our office at the Coliseum. Coming from California, I knew a thing or two about being hot. But there was nothing like that office in the Coliseum. I used to drape myself over the tiny air conditioning unit in the window in search of some sort of relief. That room is now a storage closet.

Part of what informed the volleyball team's practice philosophy was gained by venturing out from our closet-masquerading-as-an-office and making the short walk to Memorial Stadium. One of the things Nebraska football was famous for was its four-station practice. In an era before scholarship restrictions, Nebraska could be known to have 150 players on the football team, if walk-ons were included. That's a lot of people to manage in a two-hour window. Osborne and his assistants would run four stations during each practice, meaning the first through fourth teams were all working on something all the time. The 150th player was getting nearly as many reps at practice as the best player.

Pettit and I watched that and thought to ourselves, "Why can't we do that for volleyball?" It became part of our daily plan, and if you watch Husker practices today, you will see us running three courts at one time. Each player is working on something. There's no standing around while the first team gets the majority of the coaches' time. It is even more valuable in volleyball, considering that you may need your 15th-best player far sooner than a football team will reach the end of its bench.

We did not lose a conference game during my three years as an assistant at Nebraska, advancing to the regional semifinals of the NCAA Tournament twice and going all the way to the championship match in 1989, where we fell to Long Beach State in 3 sets. There was a familiar face on that Long Beach State team—Tara Cross. She had joined the 49ers' program to play for coach Brian Gimmillaro, who was also her high school coach during her sophomore and junior years at Gahr High School. Tara had now kept me from winning two titles: a state championship in high school and a national championship as an assistant.

One of Pettit's favorite sayings during those years was, "The day you stop learning something at Nebraska volleyball, that's the day you're ready to go somewhere else and be a head coach." My situation was a little different. I did not leave Nebraska for another head coaching job, at least not directly. I left following the 1990 season to join the U.S. Men's National Team as an assistant coach as it prepared for the 1992 Olympic Games in Barcelona, Spain. But through a unique set of circumstances, I also accepted the head-coaching job at the University of Wisconsin despite the fact that I was already committed to being in Spain for the Olympics that August.

While I could not start any job until I returned from Barcelona, I was considering two options: Wisconsin or Arizona. There was a sizable difference between the two programs at the time.

Arizona had been to the NCAA Tournament nine out of ten years in the 1980s, but by the end of the 1991 season the Wildcats had bottomed out, going 4-26 and winless in Pac-10 Conference games. The team still had a history of success and there was young talent on that team. But it just did not have the right coaching fit.

Wendy and I took two visits to Tucson, looking at houses and getting wined and dined by the athletic department on our second trip. I was ready to call them up and tell them to start drafting a contract. "Okay, we're taking the Arizona job," I said to Wendy after our second visit. "It's six hours from San Diego by car, only an hour-long flight, all of our family is out here, and it's warm."

The Wildcats' program was poised for a quick turnaround, too. I knew it. In my sales pitch to Wendy, I told her that whoever took the job would win a coach-of-the-year award within five years.

It was not persuasive enough. Wendy had fallen in love with the more traditional college-town life she had just experienced in Lincoln. "You're taking the Wisconsin job," she said. "I'm not raising our kids out here in the cactus and the sand. I want a two-story house and a big lawn with a tree on it."

That was persuasive enough. Madison is sort of the epitome of a classic college town and it offered a nice life for our family. But the Badgers' program was in a much different place at that point.

Wisconsin began competing in women's volleyball in 1974 and it took thirteen seasons before the Badgers recorded a win over a ranked team. Steve Lowe, a friend of mine from the coaching circuit, was the man responsible for engineering the turnaround. He took the Wisconsin job in 1986 and by 1990 he had led the Badgers to a Big 10 title and the program's first NCAA tournament appearance.

Lowe could have stayed in Madison as long as he had wanted at that point, but tragedy struck in the summer of 1991. A nonsmoker, Lowe died of lung cancer at age thirty-five, just weeks before the season started. Wisconsin promoted one of Lowe's assistants, Margie Fitzpatrick, to coach a team that had six seniors returning and was coming off the best season in program history. Fitzpatrick led that team to the regional round of the NCAA Tournament. The Badgers' draw in that round? Nebraska, which beat Wisconsin in 3 sets.

I was not there for that match, having left following the 1990 season to begin my work with the U.S. Olympic Team. A few months after that Nebraska-Wisconsin match, I agreed to take over the Badgers' program. It was going to be a whirlwind summer. I was scheduled to be in Spain with the Olympic Team through August 9, at which point I would fly straight to Madison and start preparing for a new season. Ready or not, I was going to be a head coach at the college level. Arizona found its coach, too.

David Rubio ended up taking that job and he was still there in 2016, twenty-five years later. He led the Wildcats to a 10-17 record in his first year in 1992. In 1993 Arizona went 20-11 and advanced to the Sweet Sixteen of the NCAA tournament. Rubio was named the AVCA West Region Coach of the Year. Meanwhile, I was in Madison enduring the coldest winter of my life.

2

Culture Drives the Dream

> "If you want to win in the future, you must win the grind today."—URBAN MEYER, Ohio State football coach

I was kicked out of my own locker room at Wisconsin's Field House, just 4 matches into my tenure coaching the Badgers. There was nothing I could do about it: when a rock star like Bono wants your locker room, Bono gets your locker room. Simple.

That happened during the Isthmus Badger Classic in 1992, the first tournament of my time at Wisconsin and the first games I coached in front of what would be my home crowd for the next seven years. I had only been in Madison for a month at that point, flying straight there from Barcelona, where I had helped coach the U.S. Men's National Team to a bronze medal in the Olympics. Four weeks later we were hosting three teams in a tournament: Bowling Green State, twenty-fifth-ranked Kentucky, and fourth-ranked Pacific.

We lost our first match to Kentucky on Friday. On Saturday we were scheduled to play the other two teams, first Bowling Green State and Pacific second. We could not get into our locker room that day because U2 was scheduled to play a concert on Sunday at Camp Randall Stadium, the Badgers' football stadium adjoining the Field House. This was the Zoo TV Tour, perhaps one of the most expensive and ambitious rock shows in history up to that point. A band and crew do not just roll into town the day of and set up an eleven-story stage with four massive video screens. The entourage gets there the day before.

We were allowed into the Field House to play the matches and that was about it.

U2 played to more than sixty-two thousand fans that September 13, 1992. Wisconsin's football team, Camp Randall's permanent occupant, only averaged about fifty-three thousand in attendance the previous season. We drew a total of twenty-five hundred fans for all three matches, and we lost every one of them.

While I was out of a locker room for a day, I was happy to even have enough players to play. Part of the reason we were facing two Top 25 teams that weekend was because of coach Steve Lowe's success prior to my arrival. Because he had built Wisconsin into a program capable of winning a conference title, the schedule had started to reflect the Badgers' rise up the volleyball ranks. If a program wants to play with the best, it has to schedule the best.

But we were nowhere near ready to compete at that level. Lowe's death weeks before the 1991 season put a serious strain on the players and the program. Interim head coach Margie Fitzpatrick had filled in admirably during that year, but recruiting coordinator duties had become the responsibility of a graduate assistant. Six seniors had graduated from the 1991 team and we barely had enough players to scrimmage when I arrived in August of 1992. We held open tryouts. If anyone wanted to play for the Badgers and had college eligibility remaining, they were more than welcome to come and give it a shot.

That's how we found one of our best players in those first few seasons at Madison. Joanna Grotenhuis was an outside hitter from Juneau, Alaska, who showed up to one of our tryouts. Joanna had played a year of junior-college volleyball at Southwestern Oregon Community College in 1990. Then she had a baby.

When she walked into our open tryout her body was, understandably, not in what you would call "game shape." But Joanna showed us something else during that tryout. She had a bit of a chip on her shoulder and that is what we needed to get this program moving in the right direction.

Joanna only played in 12 sets that first year; we went 14-17 and finished seventh in the Big 10. Considering how late we added Joanna to the team, however, she was essentially playing herself into shape. The next year, 1993, Joanna really started to emerge as a good player but she was still somewhat stubborn. There were times she resisted being coached.

I remember a match in the Field House that season, Joanna's junior year, against Michigan. She kept missing an assignment. I told her during a timeout that if she missed it again she was on the bench. The very next play, Joanna blew the same assignment—to take the hitter she was assigned to take—so I subbed her out. When she reached the bench she grabbed one of the folding chairs and threw it up into the stands. Luckily there were only about thirteen hundred people there and no one was hurt. I immediately sent her to the locker room and the administration suspended her for the following match.

I was good friends with Michigan's coach at the time, Greg Giovanazzi. He was coaching with the U.S. women at the same time I was coaching with the men, so we went back a ways. After the game, which we won in 3 sets, he shook my hand and said, "I loved that; I wish our players would do that."

I, too, took it as a positive sign, and perhaps one of the earliest that the culture we were after was starting to develop. It was the mindset that every match matters. We want to win. We are going to fight. Joanna did not show that passion in an appropriate way, but it was clear that she cared.

Joanna would go on to lead us in kills that season, including 28 in a sweep of South Florida in the first round of the NCAA Tournament. Hers is still the three-set school record for kills and that season started a streak of sixteen consecutive winning seasons at Wisconsin. A year later Joanna again led the team in kills and was named First-Team All-Big 10. Her transformation as a player is still one of my proudest moments as a coach.

Joanna's example would go on to be one of the building blocks for the culture we tried to create in those early years at Wisconsin. At Nebraska, Pettit had taken great care to create the culture he thought played to that program's strengths, and you could not argue with the results. By the time I arrived at Lincoln in 1988, that culture was set. It was the same when I joined the U.S. National Team, which was coming off back-to-back gold medals as it headed into the 1992 Olympics. Together these made it pretty clear to me that the teams with the strongest cultures tended to win the most. I knew we had to have it at Wisconsin, but this was my first attempt at building it from scratch at this level.

Culture is something that cannot wait with any new venture. It would have been easy to get to Wisconsin fresh off the Olympics, look at what we had, and start thinking in terms of a three-, four-, or five-year plan. That sort of long-range goal setting has value, too, but when it comes to culture there is usually no time to waste. It starts on day one.

We barely had a full roster, much less a roster stocked with players handpicked to run our preferred system. But I knew we could be tougher than our opponents. Toughness was something we could control, and I knew just where to look.

I grew up across San Diego Bay from the Naval Amphibious Base in Coronado, California, so I have always been infatuated with the Navy SEALs and their methods have become a big part of my coaching ideas. Is there a better example than the SEALs of teamwork and toughness? I have not found one. So I liberally stole from their workouts. It was not uncommon to come to the Field House during those early weeks and see our team running around the gym carrying barbells over their heads, doing full-court bear crawls, or running stadium steps until their legs turned to jelly.

The regimen was not necessarily about conditioning, though that certainly was not a bad side effect of all that SEALs-inspired work. It was about creating in practice the mentality we wanted to see in matches. It was about showing our players that they were capable of more than they had ever imagined, if they were willing to ask it of themselves.

We found some kids who could embrace that mind-set. We lost some who could not. But I had no doubt that, as the underlying culture of our program, it was making us stronger.

That first season at Wisconsin was the first losing season I had experienced as a coach at any level. We got better, however. In year two we went 19-13, finishing fifth in the Big 10 and making it to the NCAA Tournament. In year three we were a couple of games better, 21-12, and again we made the tournament.

I had my sights set on more than just finishing in the middle of the pack in the Big 10 and making the NCAA Tournament, however. I wanted to win titles and those first few seasons clearly underscored how important recruiting would be in the overall rebuilding of the Wisconsin program. As a staff we wanted to go after the best players in the country. It was not going to be easy going head-to-head against the powers of volleyball at the time, but we were going to take our swings. We also knew we would have to find some players who were being overlooked, players who had a chip on their shoulders specifically because they were not being recruited by Penn State, Nebraska, or Ohio State. Those players were a perfect fit for the culture we were developing in Madison.

Laura Abbinante was our first big recruit. A highly regarded setter from the Chicago area, Laura agreed to visit campus for the Badger Classic, the same weekend I had to give up my locker room to Bono. I knew she could be a key part of what we were building, but I thought we had lost her before her recruitment had even really begun.

Laura's father was a high-powered corporate lawyer in Chicago and she went to a private Catholic school. Madison is not always a corporate, private school kind of town. It's more like the prototypical college town on steroids, which is to say the progressive point of view is the dominant point of view.

During Laura's visit that weekend I found myself walking with her and her father down State Street, which is the place to be for most things in Madison. I was selling my vision for Wisconsin volleyball and how Laura could help us get there when we all noticed a crowd of people approaching. It was a parade.

This is great, I think. I could not have planned it any better. Look at this perfect example of the vibrant campus life available to Wisconsin students. As the crowd drew closer we noticed the unmistakable odor of pot smoke. When the group's signs and t-shirts finally came into view we realized this is not a parade, it was a legalize marijuana rally.

I was certain Laura would go elsewhere, but we ended up getting her and she became the heart and soul of our program for the next four years. Laura led us in assists every season between 1993 and 1996 and she is still the career leader in that category at Wisconsin. She still ranks in the top ten in service aces and digs, too, and earned First Team All-Big 10 honors as a junior and senior and Second Team All-American honors in 1996.

When you are building a volleyball program, one key recruit can really set things in motion, particularly if she is a setter. They are like quarterbacks. If you have a good one, you have a chance to be pretty good.

We found another good one in Colleen Neels. A feisty five-foot-eight-inch setter, Colleen was a perfect fit for our culture. She did everything for her high school team—hit, blocked middle, passed, and set—but nobody other than Wisconsin had seemed to notice. I debated and debated about whether to offer her a scholarship, but finally pulled the trigger after attending a match during her senior year in her hometown of Pewaukee, Wisconsin, where I watched her essentially will her team to victory. We were the only school to offer. Even the smaller schools in our area, Wisconsin-Milwaukee and Marquette, passed on her.

We took her and it paid off big time. Colleen had that chip on her shoulder. She wanted to prove everyone wrong and she did. She backed up Laura at setter in 1995 and 1996 while getting into the rotation as a defensive specialist. In 1997 and 1998 she was a First Team All-Big 10 setter and our team captain her senior year, and she helped power us to the regional round of the NCAA tournament both years. In 2016 Colleen joined the Badgers' staff as its director of operations, which did not surprise me one bit.

We did not land every recruit we wanted, of course, but we tried. In 1995 I was certain we were going to land Jenna Wrobel, an outside hitter from Naperville, Illinois, who was the top-ranked recruit in the

1995 class. She took her visit to Madison and I borrowed a buddy's 1964 Corvette to pick her up from the airport. We were driving around this beautiful campus in a convertible Corvette and I was sure she would come to play for us.

Jenna picked Michigan State, which at the time was another Big 10 team on the rise. The Spartans were loaded at almost every position entering the 1995 season, but they needed a left outside hitter. Laura filled that role and more, earning Big 10 Freshman of the Year honors as Michigan State went all the way to the Final Four in 1995.

We had to face the Spartans and Laura twice that season. In October of 1995 we lost in 3 sets at East Lansing. A month later, however, they had to come to our place and were ranked fifth nationally. We crushed Michigan State 15–3 in the first set. They rallied to take the second, but we put them away in four.

Talk about a chip on your shoulder. I took the ticket stub from that match, encased it in Lucite, and turned it into a paperweight that sits on my desk today. It was our first big breakthrough at Wisconsin.

More recruits were to come as we continued to hone our culture. We hosted Penn State in 1997. The Nittany Lions had ended our season the year before in the NCAA regional in Lincoln and that 1997 team was a juggernaut. They had beaten the U.S. National Team in an offseason exhibition match and were ranked number one in the country when they visited Madison on Halloween.

The Field House crowd was insane that night. There were more than six thousand fans jammed in there, double the average match attendance that season, and they got to see us upset the top-ranked team in the country. It was the clearest evidence yet that volleyball was on the rise at Wisconsin. We finished that season 30–3 and tied for first in the Big 10.

It was all building to 1998. Part of what I had been selling to recruits like Colleen and Jenna was not just the chance to build something. We had a specific destination in mind as well. The 1998 Final Four was being held in Madison. Getting to make the school's first appearance that deep in the tournament and do it at home was the dream. The strength of our culture was how we would get there. That is something I have used throughout my coaching career. A team or a program's goals are always changing, but the culture, if it is a strong one, should not be. Culture drives the dream.

We entered that season ranked seventh in the preseason poll. Our first game that year was against third-ranked USC at a tournament in New Mexico. We lost in three sets, but won our next 15 matches in a row, including getting revenge on USC three weeks after that season-opening loss. We headed to the NCAA tournament with a 27-4 record and swept through the first and second rounds.

That sent us to Lincoln for the Pacific Regional, where we faced a tough UC–Santa Barbara team. It was nearly a disaster. One of our starting outside hitters, Marisa Mackey, sprained her ankle during the match. Our other outside hitter was arguing with the setter, whom she had played club volleyball with in high school. I literally had to separate them at one point. But somehow we pulled it out, winning the fifth set 15-13. We were one game away from playing in the Final Four in our hometown, but we were limping into that regional final.

Of course, Nebraska awaited us. All we had to do was beat the Huskers and my mentor, Terry Pettit, in Lincoln, at the Coliseum, where the Huskers had won 64 consecutive matches.

At that point I started thinking, "Okay, whatever happens, happens." We have a chance here to shock the volleyball world and change our status from an up and-coming program to one that has arrived, but it is going to take an amazing effort. We had that chip-on-the-shoulder effort we had worked so hard to build and I still look back on that game and feel we had a great chance to win it 3-0.

We jumped on Nebraska right away in the first set, building a 9-2 lead. Nebraska rallied, as we knew it would, playing on its home court, but we hung on to take the first set 15-12 behind eight kills from Jenny Maastricht. Marisa was also gutting it out. She could hardly walk on the ankle she had sprained the night before. But she played.

In the second set we built a 14-9 lead and had the Huskers on the ropes before things went south. We forced Nebraska to fend off 14 game points, but helped them along with back-to-back net violations and 5 service errors during that stretch. Nebraska took the set 18–16.

A lot of teams would have crumbled after a loss like that in a tough road environment. I will admit that a little doubt had crept in for me after that second set. I thought we had given Nebraska our best shot and it was not enough. I was not sure our team had anything left for the third set, but the team would prove that the culture we had crafted was stronger than that. We traded points with Nebraska to get to 5–5 early in the third set then finished it on a 10–4 run to win 15–9 and put Nebraska back on the brink of elimination.

We jumped out to a 3–0 lead in the fourth set before the Huskers rallied for 9 straight points. We answered with a 5-point rally of our own, but then hit wide on back-to-back attempts. That broke the game open as Nebraska finished on a 6–2 run to win 15–10.

So there we were. One set between us and everything we had been building toward in as tough an environment as you will find in college volleyball. Our team had not backed down. It was back and forth in the fifth set, reaching a 10–10 tie. There were 5 points between one of these teams and a trip to Madison (home, in our case) for the Final Four. Nebraska, with its home crowd willing it along, scored the 5. We lost, but it is still one of the gutsiest performances from any team I have coached.

After the match I went to shake Pettit's hand; I was exhausted, he was emotional. "I don't know that I've ever had this strong of conflicted feelings. I was happy as I could be and as sad as I could be for Wisconsin. I love John Cook. I've been in this situation, but I think the athletes understand and coaches understand that great competition takes two great teams," Coach Pettit told reporters after the game. "Certainly you can celebrate, but I'm just more in awe of the match, more than I am wanting to celebrate."

I, of course, was also not in a mood to celebrate as I headed back to the hotel. The end of a season always hits you hard. You cannot help but flip ahead and start thinking about what you need to do for next season. Then everything changed. My phone rang and it was Coach Pettit. "Let's meet at the Cornhusker," he said.

Wendy and I got ready and headed down to the place where I had first interviewed for a job at Nebraska a decade earlier. Coach Pettit was there with his wife, Anne, and we sat down for some food. "I'm getting out of coaching and I want you to come back," he tells me not long into the meal. I started laughing.

"What are you talking about? You're not ready to get out of this," I said.

"No, I really am." I looked to Anne, and she confirmed it. Pettit shared his plan to get me back to Nebraska. He planned to coach one more season, but he wanted me to come back as the associate head coach and then take over the program at the end of 1999. My head was spinning. A few hours earlier we had nearly beaten Nebraska, now I was being asked to take over the program in a year.

I left that meeting still in disbelief that this was even on the table, but when I got back to Madison I got a call from Nebraska's athletic director Bill Byrne. It was a real offer and the wheels were already turning.

Byrne told me they were prepared to essentially pay me a head coach's salary to be the associate head coach for a year. Coach Pettit had told me previously that Byrne was one of the best athletic directors around and he made a compelling pitch. I confirmed I was interested and that really set the wheels in motion. Nebraska needed time to get the contract offer approved, so that gave us about two months to weigh our options. It was not a given that we would go.

Wendy and I loved our life in Madison. The kids were in good schools. The Badgers were winning, right there on the cusp of a Final Four two years in a row. Madison is a great town with a great culture and I loved working alongside Barry Alvarez, a former Nebraska football player who was building Wisconsin football team into a power using the Husker model. Most of all, Wendy's instincts were correct back when we were trying to decide between Arizona and Wisconsin; Madison offered a really high quality of life and we were happy.

But we had also really loved being in Lincoln, so when I received an official offer from Nebraska in late February of 1999, I took it to our athletic director at Wisconsin and said here is what they are offering, do you want to match it? If Wisconsin had matched it we might have stayed, but I was told it could not match Nebraska's offer. I walked out of that meeting, called Bill Byrne, and officially accepted the offer.

On February 22, 1999, Nebraska announced the hire and I became the volleyball coach that gave up a head-coaching job with a team that was close to contending for national championships to become an assistant coach with a program that already was.

As I mentioned earlier, taking over at Nebraska presented a significantly different challenge than what I had faced at Wisconsin. When I went to Madison I was coming from Nebraska and the U.S. National Team, two programs with strong cultures already in place. It was easy to take that for granted. I realized quickly at Wisconsin that we were starting from scratch in that regard.

Back in Lincoln, however, the challenge became preserving what was already there while bolstering it with some of my own ideas. Some of those ideas are bedrock principles. Some of those ideas have evolved to adapt to a changing game and always new players. They will be explored here in depth, but for now there is value in boiling things down to their essence as well.

In 2016 I asked my friend Jack Riggins, a former Navy SEAL, to give me three things that described the SEALs' culture. This is what he told me:

It is we, not I. The team comes first.
Integrity. You always do the right thing. You always do what you say you will do.
You work really hard. Whatever it takes, you have to do. The team can always count on you.

If you were to ask me to do a similar punch list for the culture we have created at Nebraska, I would start with: training the complete athlete and taking a holistic approach. We have a finely honed sense of our training methods developed over years at the school that pioneered strength and condition training for college athletes. We know we can build strength, agility, and athleticism through our Husker Power program. In addition, we focus in on flexibility and stretching, and finding ways to take athletes who spend most of their day hunched over a computer or phone and make their bodies capable of executing at a high level. Beyond just the physical, however, we are also constantly thinking about the mental approach to maximizing performance. With the help of our sports psychologists, we teach our players how to mentally prepare for matches and, more important, how to build the mental strength necessary to play the best in the defining moments. Nutrition is another part of it. We do not just give our players nutritious food at the training table, we teach them how to prepare it and why it is important.

When I am out on the recruiting trail, I don't tell recruits, "Come to Nebraska and we will make you an All-American." I tell them that we can prepare them to go to Germany or Azerbaijan or Russia to play professionally if that is their dream. We will give them the tools necessary to do that and they will be fully capable of managing themselves to the same degree they were managed at Nebraska.

Perhaps the best examples of that philosophy are Kadie Rolfzen and Amber Rolfzen. "The Twins," as we called them throughout their time at Nebraska, were two of the biggest volleyball recruits the state of Nebraska has ever produced. They committed to Nebraska before their freshman year of high school and entered college with a mountain of expectations, expectations they met over four years that included numerous individual awards, as well as a Big 10 Championship and a national title. Two weeks after their senior seasons ended, the twins headed to Dresden, Germany, to join Dresdner Sportclub 1898 to begin their professional careers.

In my experience, about 50 percent of U.S. players who go overseas to play volleyball are back in the United States within a year. For players who have played volleyball at big-time programs, stepping into the professional world can often feel like moving to another planet. Where are the trainers and nutritionists? Where is the weight room? Who is making sure I am eating right and keeping my body healthy?

I knew that would not be an issue for Kadie or Amber, or any of our athletes who go on to careers after college, because we have specifically prepared them to take care of themselves while remaining elite athletes. They take cooking classes in the summer so they can prepare their own food. They typically have been overseas for a team trip, so they know what it takes to get their cell phones set up and how to exchange money. They know about the importance of getting sleep, stretching, and taking a healthy mental approach, because those are things we take great care to coach them on at Nebraska.

For players who want to go into coaching after they are done playing, they have real experience examining all of the facets of building a program. I see so many coaches who worry only about what happens in the gym and when they are out recruiting. But success is dependent on much more than that. Our players understand this because we make it a point to teach them about it. That is the complete athlete we hope to develop.

Second, we build personal relationships in an era of disconnection. It is harder now than ever to construct the type of personal bonds that used to be thought of as simply a by-product of team sports. So now we work harder than ever to ensure those bonds stay strong. Talented teams will win a bunch of matches, but the strongest teams, the teams that have developed ultimate trust among each and every player, will win the biggest ones.

Third, we build champions at Nebraska through uncommon support and unconventional and constantly evolving thinking. The program we have built at Nebraska can stand with any of the most successful programs in the sport, based on wins and championships. What sets us apart is our ability to constantly challenge the ideas that got us here and develop new ways of thinking that are suited to the athletes we are developing.

Creating a culture can feel like an enormous task, but protecting it once it is established may be an even bigger challenge. It is something we work on every day with our team and our staff. Team culture is always getting dinged. Egos get in the way. There are always questions to deal with: Who is getting more playing time? Who is getting more publicity? The players change. The game changes. Coaches change. It's an assortment of constant challenges. The good news is that it's possible to build a culture that is strong enough to stand up to all of those challenges and more, but as a coach you had better be prepared to do everything you can, every single day, to protect the culture you've built.

3

Why Nebraska?

"Good, better, best. Never let it rest. 'Til your good
is better and your better is best." —SAINT JEROME

My family and I arrived back in Lincoln in the spring of 1999. It certainly was not a common move, leaving a head-coaching job of a team on the brink of making the Final Four the previous two seasons to take an associate head-coaching job, even if it was at the place where I started my college coaching career.

Another way to put it: everyone knew what was up. The only logical reaction to the news of my hiring was that Terry Pettit was planning to retire and I was going to replace him and take the reins of the Nebraska program.

We played coy about the succession plan throughout 1999. At his press conference a day after announcing that I was returning to Lincoln, Pettit refused to confirm that he was retiring. At my final press conference in Madison, the same day Nebraska was announcing my hire in Lincoln, I also did not take the bait, instead telling reporters I had Husker blood running through my veins.

That part was true. During my first stint in Nebraska I had seen how much the sport of volleyball mattered to the people there. There is an uncommon bond between Nebraskans and the University of Nebraska, and I knew that level of support was capable of powering a program to great heights. Any coach would thrive on that support and I knew you could not find it just anywhere. Nebraska was special.

But some in the state were skeptical. I still remember Jim Rose, then the well-known host of a popular radio show in Nebraska, questioning the hire. I got a raise from my head coach's salary at Wisconsin to be the associate head coach at Nebraska. It was a significant investment in the sport at Nebraska and it certainly led to some questions. "Why are we paying this guy a head coach's salary?" I recall Jim asking on his radio program one night after I was hired. "Only four thousand people really care about volleyball here, but we're paying a ton of money."

We would regularly draw four thousand people, a sellout crowd, when we played at the Coliseum. When we moved into the Bob Devaney Sports Center in 2013 and doubled our capacity, we kept selling out. Jim is a friend of mine who now works in the athletic department at the university, but I like to remind him of that comment whenever I see him, particularly if it is at a match with more than eight thousand people in attendance. "Only four thousand people care, huh, Jim?"

Finding championship-level volleyball talent as a college coach is not any different than it is in football, basketball, soccer, baseball, or any other sport in that it's largely a function of population. The more people a place has, the better the odds of producing top-level talent. Do people really love high school football in California, Florida, Ohio, and Texas? They sure do, and that matters when it comes to the type of players that come from those states. But they are also four of the most populous states in the country. That matters too.

So how does Nebraska, a state of 1.8 million people, annually produce some of the best high school players and teams in the country? That is one of my favorite discussions and one I have thought about quite a bit.

There have been weeks during my time at Nebraska when we have not been the only team from the state ranked number one in the polls. I will get to my office on Monday, the day the polls come out, and see not just Nebraska at the top of the AVCA poll for Division I, but also see Nebraska-Kearney in the top spot in Division II, Western Nebraska Community College leading the junior-college poll, Hastings College or Midland University at number one in the NAIA, and Papillion–La Vista South or another local high school topping the national prep rankings. Not only is there enough local volleyball talent to power the Husker program, there's enough to power multiple programs in Nebraska. How does that happen?

Pettit deserves a lot of credit for creating a winning culture at Nebraska and then sharing that expertise, which lifted the sport at all levels across the state. When he led Nebraska to the NCAA final in 1986, it was the first time a team from outside of California or Hawaii had played for an NCAA title. Nebraska again was runner-up in 1989.

That success was instrumental in making volleyball matter in Nebraska, but Pettit did plenty of groundwork that went beyond just winning. He was always holding clinics throughout the state, spreading the sport. If high school coaches had questions, he was always available to answer them.

We have had some true dynasties develop at the high school level in Nebraska. Jake Moore, the longtime coach at Lincoln Pius X, tallied 705 wins and seven state titles. John Peterson won 863 matches and fifteen state titles over thirty-seven years at Columbus Scotus. Steve Morgan won more than 900 matches and took home three state titles as the head coach at Ogallala. Sharon Zavala also topped 900 wins while claiming nine state championships at Grand Island Central Catholic. The level of volleyball instruction in Nebraska has been very high for a very long time.

Of course, topflight instruction requires players to receive it, and Nebraska was better off in that regard than many people might think. The Nebraska School Activities Association began hosting a state tournament for high school girls' volleyball in 1972, right around the time girls' athletics were becoming more mainstream across the country. But the sport's history here dates to earlier than that.

During one of my early tours of the state as the Huskers' new head coach, I stopped at Ole's Big Game Steakhouse & Lounge in Paxton. It's a Nebraska institution, stuffed with the exotic hunting trophies of its original proprietor. It's the perfect place to drum up some support for the sport.

While I was there shaking hands and making conversation, a group of women approached and wanted to talk about their experiences playing volleyball. They were all in their fifties or sixties but they told me about their experience playing nine-a-side volleyball in the 1940s and 1950s at a high school in the Sandhills.

At the time I had no idea that the state's history with the game stretched that far back, but, in combination with Nebraska's success in the sport, I started to see why the sport seems to be in the DNA here. The biggest factor in making the Cornhusker State into a small-but-mighty volleyball factory, however, may be the people themselves.

Nebraskans are a hard-working bunch. Nobody disputes that. In fact, it is mentioned so often that some people outside of the state might be tired of hearing it. But I tell everyone that the adage is true. Not everyone in Nebraska farms, but many people do and those that do not are around farmers all the time. They see the work ethic necessary for that job and it seems to permeate the state no matter the vocation. You try farming for a year: planting the crops, laying out huge amounts of money, hoping for just the right conditions, and then not knowing how things will turn out. It changes people, and, in my opinion, the change is for the better.

My coaches and I have certainly found it to be true in the players we have recruited from Nebraska. In fact, we have started to identify recruits and offer scholarships based on some of what we have learned through being here since 2000.

A few years ago I did a tally of all of my Husker rosters to that point. I found that about 40 percent of my players on any given team were from Nebraska. On my first Husker team in 2000 eight of the fourteen girls were Nebraska natives and we had just about the whole state covered. Anna Schrad and Sara Westling were from Lincoln. Pam Krejci and Lindsay Peterson were from small towns south of Lincoln. Laura Pilakowski, from Columbus, and Jenny Kropp, a Grand Island native, gave us two players from central Nebraska. That first team's in-state footprint stretched all the way west into the panhandle, too.

Angie Oxley was from Ogallala, and Kim Behrends was from Chappell, a little farther west.

It is impossible to overstate how much value local players bring to our program. When recruiting in-state players, we know we are getting somebody whose dream it is to play at Nebraska. It is a really big deal for them to wear Husker red, it is a really big deal for their families, and it is a really big deal for their hometowns. All of those things add value.

The towns those players come from may be small, but it is amazing to think about how many eyes our Nebraska players have on them, how many people have seen them succeed in high school and are rooting for them to do the same at Nebraska. I think it inspires those kids to work really hard.

The best example of what I am talking about is Lindsay Peterson. She became our director of operations in 2006, a do-everything position that requires an intense attention to detail. I knew she would be great at it because she was a do-everything player for us between 1999 and 2002.

Despite playing three different positions over the course of her career—setter, defensive specialist, and libero—Lindsay left Nebraska as the school's career leader with 1,111 digs and she played 438 of 440 possible sets over four years. She was late for one practice, total.

I still remember getting that call from Lindsay telling me she was going to be late. "Why are you going to be late?" I asked.

"We've got this cow that's trying to give birth and we can't get the calf out," Lindsay said. I laughed a little to myself. It was pretty hard for me to be upset about that, so I told her to get here when she could. Lindsay delivered the calf and eventually made it back for a portion of the practice.

That tells you a lot about her level of commitment and her work ethic. As a coach, if you can find that in a recruit, you are doing pretty well. We tend to find it a lot in our homegrown players.

We have learned over the years that if we are getting a girl from western Nebraska, we are probably getting a multisport athlete and often someone who was class president or valedictorian. She may have played an instrument in the band but probably has not played a ton of volleyball by modern-day standards. That's the trade-off you make with small-school players: the club volleyball scene is not as easily accessible, just based on the distance between towns out west. But those athletes are usually involved in everything. We are getting great all-around athletes who are a little less polished from a volleyball perspective. In the past it was easier to take those athletes and get them ready to play. It is getting tougher now because there are so many more kids playing club volleyball. Club volleyball is so prevalent now that girls who play it get quite a bit farther ahead skill-wise.

Still, when asked by parents or athletes, I almost always tell volleyball players that they are better off playing multiple sports. I told my daughter, Lauren, that from a very early age. Playing more than one sport keeps young athletes' bodies healthy by varying the movements they are making on a regular basis and avoiding overuse injuries. It also teaches them how to compete in different environments. Some of our best players over the years—Dani Busboom, Jordan Larson, Christina Houghtelling—were small town, multisport athletes, and almost all of them will tell you they got more nervous before high school track meets than they did for momentous matches at Nebraska. It is hard to replicate that experience.

There is no other way to put it: we love multisport athletes. Eastern Nebraska, which includes the Lincoln and Omaha metro areas and serves as the center of our recruiting territory, offers us the best of both worlds. The club scene is flourishing there, so the players get plenty of volleyball, but most Nebraska girls are still playing multiple sports. Kadie Rolfzen and Amber Rolfzen were great basketball players and made it to state in track. Paige Hubl, a captain on our 2012 team, was a four-year starter in soccer and basketball at Lincoln Southeast High School. When we recruit out-of-state athletes, the majority of them have specialized in volleyball. They, of course, often become great college players too, but when you consider what it is about Nebraska that makes it so strong in volleyball, I think you have to consider the fact that the players here compete in other sports more often than the players in larger metropolitan areas. Their experience with teams and being a teammate extends beyond the volleyball court. That's big.

Eastern Nebraska is where we start our recruiting. It is vital to have an acute understanding of where your program resonates, so at the beginning of every recruiting cycle we start in the eastern part of the state. What can we get here? we ask ourselves. From there we move out in concentric circles. After our 50-mile ring, we have a 100-mile ring, and a 500-mile ring where we look for players. We have good connections in those areas and a 500-mile radius from Lincoln covers our entire state, plus it includes part of Texas, where we still have some success finding players thanks to our days in the Big 12 Conference, and the Chicagoland area, which is a recruiting hotbed that is fueling much of the Big 10's recent success on the national stage.

The ring is our model, but we are always open to finding the best players we can no matter where they may be. Cecilia Hall is an example. She won a national title with us as a senior in 2015 and she came all the way from Sweden to do it.

During the summer camp season many European coaches come to the United States to spend weeks working camps. They will stop by our camp, maybe swing up to Mount Rushmore, and then head down to the University of Colorado's camp. After that they will spend some time in the mountains, and then head out west to work even more camps. It is sort of a working vacation for them.

In 2010 we had a coach from Sweden working our camp. "I see all these great athletes you have," he said. "I have one and I think she'd fit in great." Next thing I know I'm talking to Cici, as we all called her, in Linkoping, Sweden. She ended up picking us over Florida.

Cici was a tremendous athlete. She had grown up with gymnastics and, at six-foot-three, could walk across the gym on her hands. She is also very intelligent, carrying a 3.5 grade-point average in biochemistry while she was here.

But she was not a great player when she arrived because the competition in Sweden was not that high. We also struggled a bit initially to get Cici to understand the opportunity with which she had been provided. In Sweden higher education is free for Swedish residents, so a full-ride scholarship did not have the same meaning for her that it did for some of our girls. I constantly hammer home this point to our players. I tell our girls that athletes in baseball and track and swimming are getting only partial scholarships, while our players are all on full scholarships. That seems to work. We have kids who would cut off their right arm to get a scholarship.

It took Cici a while to understand that, to develop her skills, and to find her place at Nebraska, but she worked hard at it. She was a great player by her senior season, ranking second on the team in blocks and hitting .300.

A few months after Cici's final season, I walked into my office to find a letter postmarked from Sweden. It was from Cici's mom, Mona, a woman I had spoken with only once in Cici's five years on campus. In the envelope was a $100,000 check with a note that simply read "Thank you." I realized we were essentially being reimbursed for Cici's education, both in the classroom and on the court. That was a first for me, but it was a very satisfying moment. It validates what we are doing at Nebraska.

Few schools have invested as much in the sport of volleyball as the University of Nebraska has. We have first-class facilities, a tradition of success, a one-of-a-kind fan following, and we play in the best volleyball conference in the country. If you are a volleyball recruit, there is a lot to like about Nebraska.

But that does not mean that there are not challenges in recruiting. We have them, just like anyone else does, and one of the biggest challenges is distance. The farther away from Lincoln we get in pursuit of a player, the more we have to fight against some of the perceptions of Nebraska.

A few years ago I was recruiting Reilly Buechler, one of the top high school players in San Diego. You might know her father, Jud, as a twelve-year NBA veteran who was a valuable reserve small forward for the Chicago Bulls during their second championship run in the 1990s. I knew Jud as a great volleyball player who I had competed against on the San Diego beaches. He went on to play basketball at the University of Arizona, and he was also an All-American in volleyball. His wife, Lindsey, was a great setter for the Wildcats and I had coached her in the U.S. Olympic Festival, a multisport event meant to showcase amateur athletes in the years between Olympic Games.

Connections matter in recruiting, so I called Jud to see if we could get Reilly out to Lincoln for a visit. "No, I don't think she wants to leave California," I recall him saying.

I decided to try and play the basketball card. "If you had a son who was this good at basketball, would you look at Kansas?" I asked.

Point made. But my question went unanswered and Reilly went to UCLA, where she became a great player. We run into this often when recruiting the top players in the country. There is a perception in some of the volleyball hotbeds like California, Texas, and New Jersey that Nebraska is nothing but cornfields, that there is nothing here.

There are a lot of cornfields here, but few people realize that, based on population alone, Lincoln is the fourth-largest city in the Big 10, trailing only Columbus, Minneapolis, and Madison. There is a lot going on in Lincoln. Still, Nebraska is the second-smallest school in the conference. For many recruits that come to visit, and particularly their parents, Lincoln offers the best of both worlds: a lively city environment with the safety and security of a small town.

Experiencing that combination requires a visit to Lincoln, so battling the cornfield perception is something we still have to fight for the top recruits. If a recruit's decision just comes down to volleyball, we know we can stack up against any program in the country. Recruiting today, however, is often about a lot of things other than volleyball and we have had to start recruiting players earlier and earlier. With the rise of club volleyball, it is just how recruiting has sped up in this era.

Back at Wisconsin, I did not offer a scholarship to Colleen Neels, who would go on to become one of the best setters in school history, until her senior season. That almost never happens today. We are recruiting fourteen- and fifteen-year-olds now, and that presents some new challenges.

One of the biggest challenges is that as a coaching staff we have to be right in our evaluations and projections. A lot can change from the time an athlete is fourteen to the time she is nineteen or twenty and really ready compete on a major college stage. We have to be as accurate as possible in projecting that change and, as a result, I am spending more time with my staff in meetings, just trying to make decisions on kids.

We also spend a lot of time thinking about what ultimately determines the decisions talented volleyball prospects end up making when it comes to picking a school. The current NCAA rules are an odd fit for this era of recruiting.

Under current rules, a recruit cannot take an official visit, meaning one paid for by the school, until her senior season has started. For many girls the recruiting process is over by that point. They have already decided.

If they want to see schools and make a decision as a freshman or sophomore in high school, they have to make those visits on their own dime. Most of the time those visits will occur in the off-season, or, more specifically, during the spring club season when major tournaments take players in the vicinity of college campuses. In most cases, any girl that verbally commits to a school that early has not even seen an actual match played at her future campus. She may have seen the facilities, heard the pitch, attended a camp, or gotten a tour of the weight room, but she has rarely seen firsthand how she will be coached.

A lot of the things that make Nebraska a special place to play volleyball—the eight thousand people packing the Devaney Center, the undying and undivided support of the state of Nebraska, the academic support and tradition of excellence in the area—are lost on a girl who is just starting high school. The biggest thing we try to sell recruits on is the commitment Nebraska has made to volleyball. That level of commitment is possible through the commitment our fans have made to our program. If the Huskers are playing, Husker fans are there, no matter what.

Every match in Lincoln has been sold out since 2001. We have hosted three Final Fours in Omaha. All three drew more than seventeen thousand fans for the championship match. Nobody draws seventeen thousand for volleyball at any level, not even the U.S. National

Team. Nebraska volleyball has truly become one of the state's treasures. There is no place where it is more important.

Our support staff is another huge selling point, from our strength coach to our nutritionists to our sports psychologists to Dennis Leblanc, Nebraska's executive associate athletic director for academics. Every year we have a closing team banquet and every year the first thing the seniors mention is Dennis and the academic support he has given them. It is like the sandhill cranes returning to the Platte River Valley each spring: you can count on Dennis getting a thank you each and every year.

That sort of stuff always resonates with the parents. They see the commitment. I have often said that if I could recruit moms, we would never lose a recruit. They always see the value of things like our student-life center or the close-knit community Lincoln offers. This is the perfect place for a mother to feel comfortable leaving her daughter.

Fourteen-year-olds are not thinking that way, however, so it puts the onus back on us as coaches to try to communicate the value of those things. It is a tough battle and it seems to get a little tougher every year. But that is the game we have to play. So much of recruiting success just comes down to a deep understanding of your strengths and weaknesses.

If we know that some of our greatest in-state recruiting successes are the result of the work ethic and passion for the program already existing in those recruits, how do we go about finding that something in every recruit we pursue, no matter where she is located?

You cannot really reproduce the passion for the program. That is largely a local phenomenon. Girls in Nebraska dream of playing for Nebraska in the same way that girls in Texas dream of playing for Texas or girls in California dream of playing for UCLA, USC, or Stanford. But we have found that you can go looking for the traits that make for a great teammate and a coachable player. It's how we landed on what we call the "60 Percent Rule."

I have found over the years that about 60 percent of our athletes are daughters of teachers or coaches. In recruiting, that is a great cue for me. If a prospect has at least one parent who is a teacher or a coach, those kids bring something different to a team. They know it is not about them. It is about something bigger than themselves.

If you grew up with a teacher or a coach, your mom or dad did not do that for the money. They did it because they care about kids. Athletes who grow up in that kind of environment have role models that make them understand what it takes to make a great team and a great teammate.

I was fortunate enough to coach my daughter, Lauren, at Nebraska from 2010 to 2012. Every day after practice she would come up and thank me or one of the assistant coaches for coaching her that day. She didn't do that because I asked her to do it. Lauren did it because she knew how much it meant to the staff members working their butts off every day.

I think back to the example of the one practice for which Lindsay Peterson was late. At that moment she was in a stressful situation making the call to me, but she was thinking about the commitments she had made, both to her teammates and to her family. Nowhere in there was she thinking about herself. Her father, in addition to being a farmer, was also a volleyball coach. Lindsay learned that behavior somewhere.

You can keep going down the list of former Nebraska greats and find the same thing, time after time. Sarah Pavan, a three-time conference Player of the Year and the 2006 National Player of the Year as a junior at Nebraska, grew up with a father who was a math teacher and coached volleyball and badminton in Canada. Christina Houghtelling, a two-time All-American and the 2005 National Player of the Year, has a dad who coached football in Cambridge, Nebraska. Jordan Larson, a member of the 2016 U.S. Olympic Team and the first player in Big 12 history to win Player of the Year and Defensive Player of the Year honors in the same season, had a mother and stepfather who coached and her father was a teacher. Jill McWilliams, the best team captain I ever coached and a member of my first team at Nebraska in 2000, grew up in Des Moines, Iowa, the daughter of a high school teacher. The 60 Percent Rule rarely steers us wrong at Nebraska. We believe in it enough to make it part of our recruiting strategy.

4

Training the Complete Athlete

"Each day when we come to work we are trying to go from
good to great to unstoppable."—TIM GROVER, NBA trainer

For a young coach who was keenly interested in strength and conditioning training, there were few better places to be than Nebraska
when I arrived in 1988. That was thanks to Boyd Epley.

Boyd is viewed as the father of modern strength and conditioning.
He was the first paid strength coach in the country, earning that des-
ignation in 1969. The story goes that Tom Osborne, then an assistant
coach, noticed Boyd, a pole vaulter on the Nebraska track team, sitting out his senior season with a back injury but helping the injured
Husker football players with lifts and exercises in the weight room. Up
to that point, weight training at Nebraska and every other program in
the country was mostly up to the individual athlete. But Osborne saw
the skill Boyd had for instruction. The two put their heads together
and decided to approach head football coach Bob Devaney, to see
if he would create a position for Boyd and let him train the football
team. Devaney agreed and, in typical fashion, had a joke to punctuate
Boyd's historic hiring: "If anyone gets slower, you're fired."

Nobody got slower. Boyd built his Husker Power program into the
model for nearly all of the strength and conditioning programs that
came after it. The Nebraska football team made huge gains in the
weight room and those gains quickly became evident on the field.
Many of the assistant strength and conditioning coaches that worked
under Boyd were hired away to run their own programs at major col-

leges or in the pros. If you wanted to be on the cutting edge of strength training, Nebraska was the place to be.

I could not wait to get there in 1988, partly because of the chance to learn under Boyd. I still remember walking into Nebraska's recently expanded weight room that year—it was already the largest in the world—and seeing a giant platform in the middle of all the equipment, some of it designed by Boyd himself. It was right in the middle of the room. You could not miss it, and that was the point.

The platform was reserved for the athletes who had met certain scoring benchmarks in the performance index. Among the many innovations Boyd made, the performance index is one of his best known.

Created in conjunction with Mike Arthur, an assistant strength coach, and Chris Eskridge, a renowned criminal justice professor at Nebraska who helped with the math and the development of a computer program for tracking results, the performance index essentially put all athletes on the same scale and provided a universal means for comparison. Everything was based on body weight and body composition, and those are used to determine an athlete's one-rep max in specific exercises or lifts. Say a 225-pound athlete bench-pressed 315 pounds three times. Based on that, the system would calculate the most that athlete could bench press and turn out a numeric score of, in this case, 503 points. The beauty of the performance index was that it gave you a way to compare the ability and athleticism of a bulky 240-pound middle linebacker with a long and lean wide receiver.

The only way to get to lift on the podium was to hit a certain point total in four tests. For football it was the ten-yard dash, the pro-agility run, the bench press, and the squat. I thought the whole system was great and immediately wanted to install it for volleyball. What if we could compare that middle linebacker to a middle blocker?

As an assistant coach at Nebraska I worked with Boyd to develop a similar system using the same mathematical formula, but we tweaked the tests to better suit what we needed our volleyball athletes to do. We chose to measure our players in the ten-yard dash, pro agility, standing vertical, and approach vertical, that is, seeing how high a girl can touch with a three-step approach to spike.

That was in the late 1980s, and the performance index is still a big part of how we train our athletes today. We keep doing it this way for two reasons: to set goals for our players and to know if they are getting better as their careers progress.

We have what we call the 2,000-point club, and we test our athletes twice a year, once in March and once in August. To make it in the 2,000-point club an athlete has to score at least 500 points in all four of the tests. That is elite-athlete status and it is a big, big deal to hit it. When Lauren hit 2,000 points she went nuts, screaming and yelling. You would have thought she had won the lottery.

That is the feeling we have actively cultivated at Nebraska. We want it to mean that much. We want to have to have the conversation I had with Kadie Rolfzen and Amber Rolfzen before their senior seasons in 2016. They are two of the best athletes we have had at Nebraska regardless of sport, and I had to give them my Usain Bolt speech. The Jamaican sprinter and nine-time Olympic gold medalist has obliterated all kinds of records, and it's easy to get caught up in the races everyone gets to watch. But Bolt is not setting a world record every day. I told Kadie and Amber that their improvements would be on a similar scale, that is, getting smaller and smaller, but we were still going to press them to make them.

The performance index provides an easy way to understand and see those gains. For younger players we might offer the following feedback: "You scored a 1,400 this time, your goal should be a 1,600 the next time we test." This mentality provides a clear goal and applies a little pressure. If an athlete is not making gains there are only two explanations: either the program's not working(though we know that it does) or the athlete is not working hard enough.

The rest of it comes down to internal motivation. Seeing a teammate touch ten feet in the approach vertical for the first time, or hit the time necessary in the ten-yard dash, to come up with a 500-point score sets off such a celebration during testing that all of our athletes cannot help but want to get there. That is exactly what you want as a coach.

Long before the glory days of setting new personal bests in the performance index, however, are the days of work to get there. Our off-season program is still basically Boyd's design. It is an eight-week program—held once in the winter and once in the summer—broken into two four-week blocks, the first of which is sort of infamous in Nebraska circles.

It is called the metabolic circuit, and it is infamous because it is incredibly intense but also because Boyd's decades of research show that this is when the biggest gains are made. To do the circuit we put players in pairs and set a timer for 80 seconds.

The first player does a set of ten, and when the timer sounds, the next player is up. We do squats first, lunges second, then something called the push-pull on a machine designed by Boyd, three sets of each lift. After that it is biceps, triceps, and the jammer machine, another of Boyd's creations. The athletes do 80 seconds on, 80 seconds off, and the circuit takes about 45 minutes to complete. We do that two out of four days during our first four-week block of off-season training. If you ever want to see what total exhaustion looks like, come to the Nebraska weight room, which was specifically designed for this, on circuit day.

After four weeks of that, the results are pretty amazing. You can see the players' bodies change. They are forced to dig so deep to get through the circuit that their bodies almost cannot help but build muscle.

The second four-week block is more of a quick twitch–type program. We like to change it up every four weeks because we want our athletes' bodies to get shocked a little bit and have to adapt. Mentally the players also need something fresh.

We have used this approach to off-season training, formulated by Boyd long ago, since I returned to Nebraska in 1999, and it still serves us well today.

By the time I left Nebraska following the 1990 season to join the U.S. Men's National Team, I had a good understanding of what cutting-edge strength and conditioning training looked like. But I was about to expand my knowledge even more in San Diego.

You might think that a national team has cutting-edge facilities at its disposal, but it was nothing compared to what I had just left at

Nebraska. When I got to the national team it was practicing at the Federal Building in San Diego's Balboa Park. We lifted at a rented weight room we found in nearby Mission Valley. To add to the challenge, we had a wide range of athletes in the program. Some of our guys were twenty-two-year-olds and some were thirty-five. We were only eighteen months out from the 1992 Olympics and I was in charge of developing a program to get that group in top condition by the time it headed to Barcelona.

I had already been working on just that sort of long-term training plan as part of my graduate studies at San Diego State. The plan I developed for my degree served as our basic road map to Barcelona and I partnered with two local legends in the San Diego fitness community to help hone it to a fine edge.

The first was Phil Tyne. He was the San Diego Chargers' strength coach for a decade and had worked with 1984 U.S. Olympic men's volleyball team. The second was Pete Egoscue, a former marine who was wounded in Vietnam—an event that would go on to shape his entire training philosophy.

Pete's philosophy is based on posture therapy and some of his stuff is pretty out there. He is a self-taught anatomical physiologist, which may be why some medical doctors sort of look down their noses at his methods. Even so, we hit it off and I was interested in outside-the-box ideas if I could see that they worked.

I first met Pete through the golf business, where he had worked with two titans of the sport, Jack Nicklaus and Arnold Palmer. Pete's ideas were a natural fit for golf because they are all based on balance. Picture the eight major load-bearing joints in the body: the shoulders, hips, knees, and ankles. Pete's school of thought is that each of these four sets of two joints are designed to be aligned horizontally, that is, one shoulder shouldn't be lower than the other, one side of the hips shouldn't be rotated out, and a person should always be standing on two feet. Viewed from the side, all of those joints should also be aligned vertically. Injuries or pain can occur when the body is out of that alignment. Pete developed more than four hundred stretches and exercises meant to work the muscles that hold the bones in alignment.

We took some of Pete's alignment ideas, some of Phil's strength and conditioning ideas, plus some of my own ideas, and formulated a plan for the national team. One of our advantages at that time was that we could coach those athletes essentially year round. Today's national team players are all involved in professional seasons around the world, but we had access to our guys for the entire lead-up to Barcelona. We were able to finely tune our cycles in the hope of peaking in August; that team ended up winning an Olympic bronze medal.

I still use pieces of what I took from Pete, specifically some of his ideas on pregame warm-ups, and his ideas on posture and alignment have remained one of the cornerstones of our training regimen. We even consult with a local physician in Lincoln, Ron Hruska, who employs some similar methods with a focus on posture. Both Pete and Ron have saved us on occasion over the years with their unique ways of looking at things.

Cris Hall was one of our best athletes during my first stint at Nebraska as an assistant. An outside hitter from Chanute, Kansas, I watched her dunk a basketball once, and this was the late 1980s. That was freakish athleticism for the time and she eventually became an All-American in track and volleyball at Nebraska.

At one point in the middle of her career Cris hurt a disc in her back. The typical treatment at the time for an injury like that was surgery, but I already knew Pete by then, so I called him. He said, "Get her on a plane and get her out here to San Diego."

Before I could do that, I had to get it approved through Nebraska's staff. I thought they were going to kill us. Here was this outside-the-box treatment and they were understandably skeptical. But Bill Byrne was open to it, so we put Cris on a plane and sent her to Pete.

She was in San Diego for three days. Pete examined her and put her through some intensive stretches and exercises. When Cris got back to Lincoln she said it was the hardest three days of her life, but she did not miss another match.

Ron is capable of taking things to a different level. He has a physical therapy degree from the University of Nebraska Medical School, so, in addition to posture and alignment, he looks at things like bite, vision, breathing, and hearing. Those are things people are not typically thinking about when it comes to athlete injuries, but they all have the potential to be the root cause of something bigger. Ron has had numerous successes with our girls over the years, but perhaps none more notable than what happened with Hannah Werth in 2009.

If you want to talk about an athletic family, Hannah's is it. Her father, Dennis Werth, played Major League Baseball, as did her uncle, Dick Schofield, and her grandfather, "Ducky" Schofield. Hannah's mother, Kim Schofield Werth, was a track star at Florida who competed in the 1976 U.S. Olympic trials in long jump and sprints. Her brother, Jayson Werth, played his fifteenth season in the majors in 2016. Hannah has the same genes and was an explosive athlete for us right from the start, earning AVCA National Freshman of the Year honors in 2009.

In the offseason between Hannah's freshman and sophomore years we started to notice a problem. She started getting stress fractures in her foot. We put her through our normal battery of tests. We checked her nutrition. We tried different shoes. Nothing worked, so we went to Ron.

It was not long into his examination before he said, "It's not her foot, it's her vision." Ron had noticed that Hannah had a scar on her jaw and asked her about it. She told him she had been a figure skater and, once when she was eleven years old, she was practicing and went into a sit spin. A nearby skater, skating backward, raised her leg to go into a spin, didn't see Hannah, and her skate clipped Hannah right on the jaw. An inch or two lower and things could have been much worse, but the injury was bad enough: it shaved off part of her jaw bone and required fifty stitches.

Hannah recovered and continued to skate for a while before giving up the sport in favor of volleyball. When Ron heard the story of that injury, however, he decided to check Hannah's vision. He determined, in coordination with the athletic department's athletic medicine staff, that Hannah's long-ago injury had left her with an undiagnosed vision shift and that was the source of her stress fractures.

Basically when Hannah jumped and then looked at the floor to land, what she was seeing as the floor wasn't actually there. She was bracing to land before she was hitting the ground, which resulted in her coming down harder than she should have been. We got her fitted with some corrective goggles, she started seeing the floor, the stress fractures went away, and Hannah went on to earn All-America honors as a sophomore, junior, and senior.

Over the years we have had plenty of examples like that and it has shaped how we approach training. It helped us arrive at what we call "prehab" at Nebraska. If rehab is all about recovering from injuries, prehab is about preventing them to the greatest degree possible.

Doctors are trained to go in and fix health problems. If your car breaks, the mechanic goes in and fixes it. We want to always be thinking about what we can do to avoid the trip to the doctor or the mechanic altogether. For your car, you get the oil changed, have regular maintenance checks, and stay up on everything. Our prehab program is not much different. We do not want to get to the point where a doctor has to fix something. To do that, you have to think about how your athletes are walking into the gym every day.

I was very involved with our strength and conditioning training at Nebraska until 2005. That year I was approved to hire a strength coach devoted solely to volleyball, and I chose Laura Pilakowski. Not only was she a former player and an All-American for our team, she was also the Husker Power Lifter of the Year during our national championship season in 2000.

Laura did a great job for us but eventually left coaching to focus on her family life, so I was left looking for a replacement. Around that time I had noticed a new addition to the strength and conditioning staff at Nebraska. Brian Kmitta came to Lincoln in 2009. He was training with the track team at the time as well as working with former Nebraska wrestler and Olympic gold medalist Jordan Burroughs. I kept noticing his work and I liked how he trained, so I brought him on board. In recent years he has even been able to travel with us on occasion, which leads to an even closer connection with the team.

Prior to hiring people like Laura and Brian, whenever I wanted something done on the training end of things I had to do it myself.

Having full-time coaches available has allowed me to think about strength and conditioning on a broader level. As a result, our training plan at Nebraska has changed for the better in recent years.

In today's age we know that our players are going to spend most days sitting at a computer. We know that they're going to be hunched over their phones, texting. We know they're going to have their headphones on all day, maybe right up to the minute practice begins.

To take those players straight from that environment to one in which we are asking them to run and jump for three hours, to start spiking volleyballs at 50 or 60 miles per hour, does not make a lot of sense. Our job, then, is to put their bodies in a position where they can go in and do what we are going to ask them to do. We want to take them from the dysfunctional positions their bodies are in all day and put them in functional positions before we start practicing. This is more than simply stretching a muscle before you use it. This is about aligning joints and getting the body back to the way it was designed to work before modern life intruded. Pete will often use the example of primitive man when describing functional bodies. The bodies of hunter-gatherers had to be ready to go at all times. Whether confronted by predator or prey, they did not have the luxury of stretching before they needed to move. They always had to be ready to hunt, gather, run, or fight.

We know our players' are not in that state after a day of classes and studying, so it is imperative that we get them ready before workouts begin. We do not expect practice to be the process through which the players work out the kinks of a day spent in a chair. We have a battery of exercises, designed by Pete and Ron, that do that and they are all part of our effort to train complete athletes. This is the start of the prehab process, and it is all about putting players' bodies back in their most functional position so they are ready to practice at a high level.

It begins first thing Monday morning of a game week. Brian will monitor the players as they go through their core lifts, cleans, and squats, so they are maintaining their strength throughout the season. He will also have an individualized plan for exercises each player needs to do based on what we will be asking her to do that afternoon in practice.

We have noticed over the years that our middle blockers pull their abdominal muscles more often than players at other positions, so our middle blockers do stretches and exercises to strengthen the core. Setters are running all over the court during a match and setting the ball from about every angle imaginable. To be able to do that, they need to be well-balanced. We want to get setters back to a balanced position the day after a match, so we might have them doing medicine ball workouts on a trampoline, which forces them to find balance. Outside hitters are exerting a lot of torque on their bodies over the course of a match, so they may have stretches designed to bring their pelvises into alignment.

One of Boyd Epley's key ideas in training is the push-pull method. That, in its simplest form, means working the body equally on both sides. We are constantly conscious of that in training as well.

Our 2016 team, for example, was entirely right-handed. On game day every girl on the team was serving, hitting, playing pepper, and swinging her right arm hundreds of times, and it's all a one-way motion. Part of our plan in the days following the match was designed to work the muscles on the left side of the body a little more strenuously to pull bodies back into balance. We want symmetrical athletes. That is the goal.

Everything starts with balance, which extends beyond just how we are asking our players to train. We are also constantly preaching something we call the mind-body balance. If an athlete does not know how to handle stress, her body is going to break down, her mind is going to break down, and her whole system will break down. We see it in all different forms with our players—the stress of school, the stress of relationships, the stress of daily life, the stress of playing almost every game with a target on our back. We have to have a plan in place to deal with it.

We are lucky at Nebraska to have an athletic psychologist available to us. Initially Dr. Larry Widman filled that role for us and now

Dr. Brett Haskell works with athletes across all twenty-four sports at Nebraska. I am constantly looking for ways to embed her more fully with our team. In 2016 she traveled with us on select road trips for the first time and we have seen that the players really count on her expertise.

Haskell has pointed us in the direction of problems that we may never have seen coming. For example, we have major sleep issues. One of the things we know about today's athletes is that they do not sleep well. They have trouble shutting down after workouts and they struggle shutting down after staring at a screen all day. We now monitor our players' sleep using wearable technology called Readibands. This is same technology worn by the Chicago Cubs when they won the World Series in 2016, the club's first title in 108 years. The Seattle Seahawks implemented it in 2011 and won the Super Bowl in 2013.

Developed by a company in Vancouver called Fatigue Science, the bands measure a player's heart rate and length and quality of sleep, as well as how much they recovered from the day before based on those factors. The players do not have to do anything other than wear the bands. When they come to the practice facility the data from the day before is automatically uploaded wirelessly. Each player gets a printout depicting their sleep from the night before. The program, based on a model developed by the U.S. Army to measure how sleep correlates with performance, spits out a recovery percentage. One player may have recovered at 70 percent, another at 85, and so forth. The players all know they cannot cheat the system.

We use that data to do a couple of things. First, we can look for trends. Do we have players who are consistently getting too little sleep? If we know it, we can address it. Second, we can use what we know to determine how to practice. If everyone on the team is coming off a late flight home from a road game, maybe we go a little lighter in practice. When we faced Penn State at an 11:00 a.m. match in the 2016 NCAA tournament, I decided to skip our typical serve-and-pass warm up, which would have required the players to be at the gym at 6:00 a.m. Based on the data, it was apparent that the value of sleep outweighed the value of routine.

We also spend a lot of time talking about breathing exercises. Much like the way modern life creates dysfunctional bodies, sitting slouched over at a desk all day really taxes the respiratory system as well. We try to address that through breathing exercises. We also talk about meditation. I clearly recall asking Tom Osborne once how he dealt with stress and I was shocked to learn that he meditated every morning. (That was after he reminded me, somewhat jokingly, that he'd had heart surgery at age forty-seven.)

I knew the benefits of meditation. I, too, meditate each day. Some of my best motivational ideas or strategy tweaks come when I'm on my bike or on a long walk with Wendy and the wolfhounds. But Coach Osborne? He is about as salt-of-the-earth as they come and he made his name in the rough-and-tumble world of college football. Yet he finds value in what some still consider a new-age technique.

That was all the evidence I needed to really ramp up how much direction we were giving our team on the mental side. We have tried to instill the idea that you have to be able to quiet the mind. Great athletes know how to quiet the mind. That part is very important to how the body performs. There's a connection there, so some of our players are taught to meditate and some are given specific breathing exercises to try.

This, too, is partially a response to what we see in the athletes we coach now. Brett will tell you, too, that the number one issue that players of this generation struggle with is not knowing how to deal with failure.

The youth sports system has developed to identify the best and brightest earlier and earlier, particularly in volleyball. The type of athlete we are recruiting has often been the best player on every team on which she has ever played. There are a enough teams out there that if she finds out she is not the best player on the team, more often than not she will find a new team where she can be the best player. When adversity hits for those players, and inevitably it will, it will often feel like a totally foreign experience. The danger then becomes what they are telling themselves to get through it. Negative self-talk is the enemy.

Part of what we are stressing with the mind-body balance is for our players to have positive self-talk going on and to think positive rather than negative thoughts.

To drive it home, we tell our team that the average person has around sixty thousand thoughts a day. They should ask themselves how many of those thoughts each day are positive and how many are negative. It is a simple message, but it has helped us maintain an awareness of how our minds work.

We are constantly educating our players that if you want to perform really well on the court and in the classroom, you have to first look at your mind and then be willing to work on your mind. This means quieting it down, being able to recover, having quiet time each day, and paying attention to your breathing.

The last major component of our overall training program is nutrition. Like most major college programs we have a training table for scholarship student-athletes and give them access to nutritionists, but occasionally old habits are hard to break.

Christina Houghtelling was a great outside hitter for us from Cambridge, Nebraska. Early in her career she was dealing with stress fractures in her tibia. This is a weight-bearing bone and an incredibly rare place to get stress fractures, so we had a hard time determining why they were happening. We decided to do a bone density test.

What we learned was that Christina had basically never eaten a green vegetable in her life. Growing up on a farm, she was as meat-and-potatoes as they come. So we got her with the nutritionists, they put together a plan for her, and every day she was eating bowls of spinach and dark green leafy vegetables. We also started giving her vitamin supplements.

It didn't take long to see the results. Christina went from a slow, injury-prone freshman to the AVCA National Player of the Year two years later. It was a magical transformation.

That is when I realized we needed to do more to address nutrition for the team. Pete Egoscue recommended I visit the Cooper Institute in Dallas. Ken Cooper, a U.S. Air Force physician who coined the term "aerobics" in his 1968 book on the topic, founded the institute in 1970 and it has remained focused on preventive medicine, which meshed well with our overall training philosophy.

By the time I got to Dallas in the mid-2000s to check it out, the Cooper Institute was deep into the study of triathletes and was enjoying success with a mineral supplement engineered specifically for endurance athletes. We had some meetings and decided to try formulating something more tailored to our non-endurance athletes.

Of course you don't just come back from Dallas and start handing out vitamins to your players. We went through a lengthy approval process with the Cooper Institute and Dr. Lonnie Albers, Nebraska's associate athletic director for athletic medicine. Eventually we got the supplements approved and they have been a part of our training program ever since. It blows my mind to think that we are the only program at Nebraska supplementing in this way.

How seriously do we take it? There is a line item in our budget for vitamins each year. We do not just give a week's supply to the players either. They have to get them when they are at the volleyball facility every day so we can ensure they are taking them. If they do not take their supplements, they do not practice.

These are the types of things we think about when trying to stay ahead in strength and conditioning. Ironically, twenty years ago Boyd Epley's efforts in this area at Nebraska made a lot of other schools realize they needed to catch up. I like to think we have maintained an edge by thinking creatively about the new challenges today's athletes face and keeping a tight focus on preventing problems before they arise.

5

Coaching the iCentered Athlete

"Learn to use your real brain, not your iPhone
brain."—JAMES OKSIUTA, magician

The world has changed drastically in the age of instant information. Not only has it changed, it seems to keep changing faster than ever before. That presents new challenges for coaches, and if you are not willing to rethink and update old ideas, even if they have always worked in the past, it is easier now than ever to get left behind.

At home is where I first noticed the changing expectations among young people. In 2008 Taylor was in junior high and one day came to me with an idea. "Hey, Dad, all my buddies are going hunting and I want to go," he said.

"Great," I said, "but I can't go. I don't know how to hunt."

"Well, I really want to do this."

"Okay, but you've got to go take the hunter safety course first." I thought that might be the end of the story. But Taylor, or "T-Man," as we call him, took the course and got his certification. I realized he was pretty serious about it.

The next thing he needed was a gun. We went to a local sporting goods store and talked to a sales associate. He showed us a bunch of different guns, made some recommendations, and Taylor picked out the one he liked.

"Okay, T-Man, it's four hundred dollars," I said. "You're going to have to save your money, do some chores, and then you can come back and buy it." A blank look came over his face. He looked at me like this was the worst news I could have given him at that moment.

"Seriously? We're not going to get this gun?"

I shook my head, but T-Man was pretty committed to this idea of going hunting with his buddies. He was not taking no for an answer.

"It doesn't have to work that way," he said. He points at an ATM near the entrance of the store. "All we have to do is go down to the ATM and we can get four hundred dollars out right now."

That was the first time it really hit me: this generation is defined by instant gratification. It is not a new term. There are newspaper references to it dating to the 1800s, but it is only in recent years that it has come to be called the "age of instant gratification," and I experienced it that day standing in a sporting goods store. It was so far removed from the experience I had growing up, when I sold cucumbers by the road if I wanted the money to buy something. It would have taken a lot of cucumbers to get a gun like that.

I decided that, even despite the helpful reminder that we had easy access to an ATM, this time things *did* have to work that way. We left without getting the gun. To Taylor's credit, he still found a way to go hunting. He borrowed a gun from the husband of one of my staff members and ended up shooting his first deer.

It would be a couple more years before I would start to notice a similar change in the athletes that were coming to play at Nebraska, and it happened on a team trip to China. I have come to call this the generation of the "iCentered" athlete, a play on Apple's famous naming convention and an acknowledgment of the effects that all those devices—which offer a constant and immediate ability to wrap yourself in a world of your choosing—have had on building a team in this modern era.

In the spring of 2000 we became the first school to send a team to China to play volleyball. It was a major undertaking just getting there, and we would not have been able to do it without the assistance of Steve Wang.

I first met Steve at Nebraska. Originally from Taiwan, Steve had worked in the restaurant business before getting a job at the university in the Department of Agriculture, where he was helping set up agreements between Nebraska and China for the trade of corn, beef, and other goods. Volleyball is huge in China, so it was not a surprise to learn that Steve was a huge fan of the sport. Once I knew that, I knew he might be able to help me make the trip I had always wanted to make as a college coach.

"Do you think we could ever get into China to play a few matches?" I asked him one day. Steve knew how to get that done.

"Let's call Lang Ping," he said. Lang Ping is volleyball royalty in China, and one of the best players the country has ever produced. She helped lead China to a gold medal in the 1984 Olympic Games in Los Angeles. She then coached the U.S. National Team to a silver medal in the 2008 Olympics, including a victory over host nation China. Eight years later she coached China to a gold medal in Brazil. If you want to organize a first-of-its-kind volleyball tour in China, Lang Ping can get the ball rolling. Once we had talked to her, things started happening.

From there I reached out to Sandy Vong, the first women's coach at Michigan and a former engineer with Ford Motor Company, who had served as an interpreter for the U.S. men's team when I first traveled with the team to China in 1991. I flew to Detroit to meet with him. He was able to put a few more pieces in place and I flew back to Lincoln with a plan to take our team to China.

Part of the reason this trip was so difficult to schedule was because relations between the United States and China were delicate at the time. I was committed to going, mostly because nobody had ever tried it before. Also, the volleyball is great there. I thought it would be a great challenge for our team, but also a perfect team-building exercise ahead of my first season as head coach at Nebraska.

Eventually we got the trip approved and away we went. In addition to our team and staff, we were also bringing Lil' Red, one of the Nebraska mascots, and a cameraman from HuskerVision, Jon Barnett, to document the historic trip.

We arrived in Beijing and before we even made it through customs, some officials noticed Jon's camera and hauled him off to a room and shut the door. I saw it happening and tried to follow, but they stopped me and told me I could not go in. The team and I were ushered through customs, but of course we were not leaving without Jon, so we just had to wait outside the airport with no cell phones and no way to know what was happening or how long we would have to wait.

After about an hour Jon emerged and he looked like he had seen a ghost. He is without the fifty-thousand-dollar camera he came in with and Steve is telling me it is unlikely we are going to get it back. With no other real options we headed for the hotel. We got there and the faucets were churning out brown water, the beds were too short for our players, and our groundbreaking trip to China was off to about the worst start imaginable.

I called Bill Byrne, and told him what had happened. He quickly reached out to Nebraska senator Chuck Hagel and Representative Doug Bereuter to see if they could assist.

A few days into the trip I got a call from Bereuter. At that point he was one of the key players in negotiating what would become the U.S.-China Relations Act of 2000, an act that eased trade between the two nations. At that moment in the spring of 2000 the United States and China were in high-level negotiations and Bereuter told me that he was going to threaten to shut down talks if the camera was not returned.

Maybe he was just posturing, but whatever he did worked. I got a call from the U.S. embassy in China and was told that the camera would be returned on a Friday. We were scheduled to fly to Shanghai on Saturday.

I waited in my hotel room all day Friday and nothing happened. I thought that was the end of it and we would once again be leaving without our camera. But early on Saturday morning there was a knock on my door. I open it to see three Chinese officials standing there. They took me to the airport, put me in a room, and gave me paperwork to sign saying we would not film anything outside of the gyms where we were playing our matches. I signed the form, got the camera, and headed back to the hotel.

Before we left for Shanghai there was one thing we had to do. Husk-erVision really wanted some footage of Lil' Red on the Great Wall. This was expressly forbidden by the paperwork I had just signed, but I decided to do it anyway. I called down for a driver, rounded up Jon, told the student wearing the Lil' Red costume to get his stuff together, and we three set out for the Great Wall. We got there, Lil' Red put his stuff on, and we filmed a quick video, all in about fifteen minutes. From there we headed back to Beijing and soon got on a plane for Shanghai.

On that flight I noticed an official-looking person sitting in a seat not too far from mine. When we got off the plane I asked Steve about it, and he told me it was a government escort sent to ensure we were not filming. Good thing he had not been trailing us a few hours earlier.

Despite the rocky start to that first trip to China, our teams made return trips in 2006, 2010, and 2014. It was on that 2010 trip that I first started to notice some iCenteredness among our players. Ironically, I was the one confiscating electronics.

The 2010 trip was the first one where our players could really stay connected. The players were using Skype to communicate back home and many of them had brought along their cell phones. It was a new dynamic and I was willing to give it a try, but we got crushed at our first few games and I noticed our bus rides were a little too quiet.

Talk about an iCentered experience: it was simply too easy for the players to plug in their head phones, disappear into whatever was transfixing them on their phones, and not have to deal with anyone or anything else. It was defeating the entire purpose of the trip and I realized that this was a huge distraction. I feared it would prevent us from building the relationships I knew we would need in order to have a truly strong team.

As a staff we decided to take the phones away. On one of the bus trips I passed around a bag and told the players to put their phones in it. They would not be getting their phones back until I noticed a change.

It did not take long. We won a couple of matches, which is never a given when you are facing professional teams in a volleyball-mad country. But the biggest difference was off the court. Our bus trips became lively. Without their phones the players really had two options:

try to sleep (not easy on a rickety bus on rough roads) or talk to their teammates, play games, and just have fun. They could get to know one another better, which, more than the chance to play some top-level volleyball and experience a new place, was the real reason for the trip. We wanted to become a tighter team and without phones we did.

After a few days we offered to return the phones but the players did not want them back. "We're having too much fun," they said. We eventually got to a hotel where we were staying for a few days and returned the phones because their parents were starting to worry that they had not heard from their daughters. But we learned an important lesson on that trip. Now we let our players set the team cell phone policy because we have found much more success with it when the rule comes from them rather than the top-down. There are times they choose not to have their phones and it is usually during a team event.

While we have found some success getting our players to put down their phones occasionally, that does not mean we don't have to battle the effects of a sped-up generation. We live in a world where everything is very short and quick. The average Google search takes just a fraction of a second. On Twitter, tweets are limited to just 140 characters. The initial appeal of Snapchat was that sent messages disappear after a short time. This is a challenge for coaches in any sport because we know that maximizing the potential of players often takes a really long time. We may have to work on something over and over again to become really good at it.

How do we approach that juxtaposition? There is no getting around the fact that repetitions matter in practice, but we have adjusted how we communicate with our players in recent years. We now try to match the ways in which they are already communicating, and that means short, quick bursts of information. If I get up on the whiteboard and start giving a big lecture on volleyball with somewhat complicated diagrams, the players start mentally checking out. You can feel it in the room.

So we try to keep everything short and to the point. We use key words and we move on. The only time we spend more than thirty seconds on any one issue is if we are watching a video, and even those have been adjusted for this new era.

I would love to sit down and watch video for an hour with our team, but it would be a waste of time. Now our video sessions usually last ten minutes and we use a format we call "five clip." Rather than watching three games, we have boiled it down five clips—look at this play, look at this play, look at this play, now here we go. It is all short bursts because that is how we have to relate to this generation. On a normal day I will tell our video coordinator to pull together two or three clips from our opponent and two or three clips from things we need to do better. That will be the extent of our film for that day.

We have found that this really helps with players' retention, but it also helps us as a staff to really simplify and think about what we are trying to accomplish with each practice. That is an adjustment for the old football coach in me. So was noticing, as time went on, that players struggled to know how to deal with failure.

Everyone knows the story of Michael Jordan getting cut from his varsity team as a high school sophomore. It is, perhaps, the most famous cut in the history of sports. I was cut from numerous teams as a young athlete. Most coaches I know have been cut at some point in their athletic careers. Those are impactful moments and I think they teach people to appreciate the work it takes to be really great.

Expecting the modern-day young athlete to understand that, to see potential value in being asked to work harder, is a big, big challenge when, more often than not, failure is something they have never experienced for themselves.

Brett Haskell has been instrumental in helping us deal with that challenge once we have girls on the team. Even so, it is a big hurdle in recruiting. Sometimes I will talk to a recruit about redshirting and I can see on her face that she is thinking: "What in the heck are you even talking about?" Most recruits have been playing their entire lives—not sitting the bench, much less sitting out an entire year. At times I think we might lose recruits because I will say that I think a player ought to redshirt. We have been really careful about having those discussions while recruiting.

Once we get a player into the program, however, we know that our culture makes those conversations a little bit easier to have. There is perhaps no better example of that than the decision we made with a sophomore setter in 2014.

This player was a blue-chip setter in our 2013 recruiting class from Papillion, just outside of Omaha. She was named the top high school setter in the country by PrepVolleyball.com and she ranked as the thirteenth-best player in the country. If anything, however, she may have been overshadowed playing on a team that featured her future Nebraska teammates Kadie Rolfzen, the fifth-ranked player in the country, and Amber Rolfzen, the two-time Nebraska Player of the Year and the eighth-ranked player nationally.

All three girls played for us as true freshmen in 2013, but the setter dealt with some injuries and was mostly a backup to Mary Pollmiller, then a junior. We went into the 2014 season thinking we would have a competition for the setter job. That is how good we thought this player was going to be. But every day during practice that August, Mary's stats were always better, so as we moved closer to the season I started to consider the option of redshirting the sophomore setter.

The week before that 2014 season started, I went into the Red-White Scrimmage virtually certain I was going to ask her to redshirt. Then she played well enough to give us second thoughts. We had our assistants draft the teams for that scrimmage and she really played well, leading the weaker team to a win in the match.

It gave us pause. But ultimately we felt that, from a maturity and leadership point of view, Mary still had the edge. We had no doubts about the sophomore's talent and we had a good idea that she was almost ready to lead. The bigger question was whether the team was ready to follow. We decided to go with the senior.

I called the sophomore in and told her I thought it would be best for her if she redshirted that year. There are not many people more competitive than this player. Both of her parents were athletes at Nebraska, so I knew it probably would not be a decision that went over really well initially, and it did not. Once we were able to get past the emotion of an admittedly big decision and talk through it, I was able to outline the rationale behind it.

Of course we were trying to put the best team on court that we could, but if that were the only criteria for the decision it would have been a much more difficult decision. When it came to whether or not it would benefit her as a player, however, we had few doubts. It was more than just a chance for her to mature as a player. I also thought it was really important to give her some separation from Kadie and Amber. She had played her entire career to that point alongside the Twins and they were such immense talents that I honestly thought she had not had a totally fair shot to develop her own identity as a player.

She resisted at first, but she eventually agreed to trust what we were telling her. As a sophomore the following season and again as a junior in 2016 she was named team captain, all because of how hard she worked during that redshirt year. She did everything within her control to make herself better and help the team get better. Her respect level among her teammates went through the roof. She could have dogged it and pouted during the season she sat out, but she took it as an opportunity and we saw a major shift in her.

Had we tried to have that conversation when this player was just coming out of high school, I am not sure things would have worked out quite as well. These are the sorts of things coaches have to be thinking about in today's game.

If you were to summarize our approach to tackling the problem of iCentered athletes, it really boils down to one thing that every coach should be doing at a minimum: P2P. P2P is short for person-to-person communication and it came from some of my conversations with Jack Riggins, a former Navy SEAL. It is now one of the bedrock principles in our program today.

I mentioned earlier about when we noticed on the 2010 China trip that our players often had a closer relationship with their phones than they did with one another. They were great at texting but poor at holding actual conversations. My response then was to remove the problem—the phones. But that was not a long-term solution, so now we are giving our players the ability to decide when they will have their phones and when they will not and we are also constantly preaching the value of P2P.

Like any team, we have issues arise between players. Whether it is an on-court or off-the-court disagreement, we always tell those players to talk through it. When I follow up with one of the players involved and ask if the issue has been resolved, I do not know how many times in recent years I have heard the response, "Yeah, we texted about it." That is not communication by our definition. Sending a text is not building a relationship with somebody, and we need great relationships.

The sport of volleyball is six people working together in 900 square feet of space. The ball is traveling at speeds that would be equivalent to a fastball traveling at 160 miles per hour. For a team to consistently handle that context it must have great communication, and great communication comes only from great relationships.

So how do you build that? There are camping trips and team retreats, but the real key is face-to-face contact. Unfortunately, it becomes more and more uncommon by the day. We have tried to make it common.

When I asked Jack about what made the bonds between SEALs so strong, he had an interesting answer. The job, of course, demands strong bonds. The difficulty of the training and the shared experience of suffering through it also builds relationships. But Jack also mentioned the value of just hanging out. SEALs do a lot of that. While there is always work to be done, some of the work involves waiting, and waiting often involves a lot of just talking to pass the time.

We now take some proactive steps to really encourage our players to simply hang out. In 2015 the Nebraska beach volleyball team went to Hawaii for a tournament. We decided to try something different while we were out there. Rather than have big team dinners each night, we decided to break the group into four groups of four, just like a SEAL team would do.

I took a group of four and our dinner lasted three-and-a-half hours. We normally had twenty people for one of our usual team dinners on the road. It's a logistics challenge. We have to find a restaurant that can accommodate a party of that size, first of all. Once we find that, we then usually have a big table in a private room and there is plenty of banter, but not a lot of conversation.

If you are all of the sudden dealing with a party of five, though, it starts to feel like a normal night out, a dinner setting everyone has experienced before. I had never seen the players talk to each other as openly and freely as that night in Hawaii. I did not even have to be there; the dinner still would have lasted nearly four hours. But I was glad I had been. A light bulb sort of went off after that.

I really believe the athletes of today crave personal interaction with each other, partly because they rarely get it anywhere and partly because their highly structured schedules do not always allow for it. They rarely get opportunities when the conversation is just allowed to flow. Instead they have weights at this time, class at that time, meetings at this time, sleep now. There is never just hangout time.

Once you sort of introduce this generation to the idea, they realize they crave it and start to look for the same opportunities on their own. I now try to have lunch with one or two players a week at our training table. The players never say no. I have yet to have anyone say, "Nope, not interested." I think the players like knowing that coach wants to have lunch with them today.

When we got back from our trip to Hawaii, we asked our players to list their favorite part of the trip. We figured it would be going to the beach or something like that. Every one of the players said it was the small group dinners. So we have continued that practice even when we are at home. I will now have four girls over for dinner during the summer, four more will go to another assistant's house, and four more to another's.

When we rebuilt the on-campus player lounge, we did it with relationship-building in mind. We are fortunate to have first-class facilities at Nebraska and if you go to the football or basketball player lounges, you will see ultra sleek man caves replete with flat-screen televisions and gaming systems galore.

I told our designer I wanted our lounge to feel like a family room and a place where the players could come in and just be themselves.

We have blankets and pillows everywhere. It's a cozy place. I will come in prior to a game and the team will be piled everywhere, which is exactly what I want to see.

Coaching the iCentered athlete presents all sorts of new challenges that did not exist five or ten years ago, but the answer to those challenges is as time-tested as they come: the best communication based on the best relationships leads to the team that is best prepared to win. Coaching for that is harder than it once was, but that only makes it more valuable.

6

The Team within the Team

"Almost everything in leadership comes back to relationships. The only way you can possibly lead people is to understand people."—MIKE KRZYZEWSKI, Duke basketball coach

When I left Nebraska for Wisconsin to become a college head coach for the first time, one of the most valuable pieces of information Terry Pettit gave me was to seek out the people that could help me hire the best people. "You need to hire people that are not like you," he told me. You need to surround yourself with people that will give you the truth, give you a different perspective, and maybe help you think outside the box.

Pettit was the one who planted the seed for what I now call the "team within the team." It is a simple enough idea—surround yourself with people who can help you and work to develop an inner circle—but it is remarkable how easy it is for coaches and leaders to forget it.

In my first few years back at Nebraska, I found I was forgetting it. We had won the national title in 2000, my first year as head coach, and I sort of went into a bunker mentality. I did not trust anybody. I was not listening to anybody. We had just won a national title while going undefeated. I thought I had it wired. Why did I need anybody?

Over the years I have found that this is a common problem among young or inexperienced coaches. When you are young or new to the job, you feel like you have to prove everything. That is exactly how I felt. I thought I had to prove something every day, to prove that I was a good coach. Ego is involved in that. You are trying to answer the "Am

I good enough?" question, and the only way young coaches can see to do that is by winning. Oftentimes what they don't realize is that the fanatical pursuit of that one goal may actually make it more difficult to reach. I certainly did not realize it.

As coaches gain experience, however, that pursuit of winning goes away. Your work becomes more about coaching: the journey of each unique team and seeing individual players develop. You begin to enjoy all of those things a lot more and they become more important than winning. Winning is still important, of course, but you stop making yourself miserable over it. I enjoy coaching more now than ever before and I am able to learn so much more about myself and my role as a coach because I am not so worried about proving myself every day.

It took a little maturity and help from my mentors to shake me out of my lone-wolf phase in those early years in Lincoln. I recall a conversation with Fred Kauffman as the real eye-opener. Fred was a lawyer and a big part of the Lincoln community, serving on numerous boards and devoting his time to many charitable organizations. He once told me he helped lead the Bible study group that Tom Osborne hosted each morning for his coaching staff through the Fellowship of Christian Athletes. I eventually asked Osborne about it and he told me that not only did he have his own team within the team while coaching, but that Fred was certainly a part of that inner circle. Jack Stark, a performance psychologist who worked with the Nebraska football program from 1989 to 2004, was a part of it too.

Those conversations jolted me into realizing that I had let my inner circle get a little lonely. I had forgotten one of the first things Terry Pettit had told me when I went off to become a Division I head coach: identify and include the people who can help you.

Over the next few years I made a big effort to start rebuilding my team within the team. The longer that I have been at Nebraska, the bigger my circle has become. The people in my circle now come from a variety of backgrounds. But the common thread connecting them all is trust. These are the people I trust to have the program's best interests at heart. They are the people who will tell me the truth. They are the people who help me evolve.

I first met Jack Riggins in 2011. Jeff Jamrog, Nebraska's director of football operations at the time, had brought Jack in to speak to the football team and Jeff sent me a text saying I would not want to miss this talk. I grabbed a pen and a notepad and headed over to the football complex.

When I got there Jack was dressed in his dress whites. Originally from Fremont, Nebraska, Jack had worked his way up to become a Navy SEAL commander and spent eight years deployed to Afghanistan. He told stories of teamwork and leadership and I was jotting things down in my notepad the entire time. At the end of his presentation Jack presented the football team with the flag he had carried with him during his deployment in Afghanistan and the team carried it onto the field with them before every home game that season.

I left that talk fired up. "This stuff is awesome," I said to myself. "This is my leadership mantra now." Not long after returning to my office, I got a text from Jack: "Can I meet you?"

"Are you serious? Yeah!" I had to have been more excited than Jack was for that meeting.

When he arrived we started chatting and he told me he had a special interest in Nebraska volleyball—he had married Kate Crnich, an outside hitter on the 1995 National Champion team. We hit it off immediately. That conversation ended with me asking Jack if I could use him as an advisor.

He was happy to do it, but there was a problem: he was headed to Germany for his job. I was not going to let an ocean and a time difference end this opportunity, however. We developed a Skype system that allowed us to hash out leadership ideas and just talk through issues I was noticing with the team. It went so well that eventually we made a habit of calling Jack in Germany via Skype and projecting it on a television in our meeting room so that he could take part in some of our team meetings.

By 2014 Jack was on leave from his military duties overseas and back living in Lincoln. Our team was headed to China again that year and I had put him on the list of possible people to go with us. I knew if we could get him embedded with the team he would have a real chance to make an impact because it can be a stressful trip for the players. That is part of the reason we go. Who knows better how to deal with stress than a Navy SEAL?

My request to have Jack go with us was initially denied by the university. The administration had security concerns because Jack was not a university employee. I called Jack and told him that he could not go. "Listen," he said, "I have the highest security clearance in the U.S. government. I am pretty sure I am not a security risk."

I thought about it for a few days and decided that it was important for him to go with us. The next day I went into the athletic department offices, told them I was paying for Jack's ticket, and he was going on the trip to China. There were still concerns and pushback, but eventually we got it approved for Jack to go as my guest. I think Tom Osborne may have made a call to get the okay. It was a big ordeal, but that was how badly I wanted help with leadership. Jack had lived it in the most stressful situations you could create for a team.

He made the trip and told me things about those players I never could have figured out on my own. One of the primary jobs of a Navy SEAL is intelligence-gathering and it showed with Jack. He knows people extraordinarily well.

The SEALs have had a big influence on my leadership style and philosophy since my earliest days at Wisconsin. But Jack provided me the opportunity to dig even deeper into those ideas. He introduced me to concepts like P2P communication and the value of small groups. He also has a very up-to-date knowledge of young people and it is vital for coaches of today to have an understanding of where their athletes are coming from, what their strengths and weaknesses are, and the best way to reach them.

The connection between the military and college-age athletes really struck home for me during a visit to the USS *Nebraska* in the early 2000s. During a trip to Georgia I had gotten the chance to visit the submarine nicknamed "Big Red" and met the sailors in charge of operating it. I was shocked at how young they were. When I got back to Lincoln I waited until we had a particularly rough practice and called our team together and told them I had seen kids their age running a billion-dollar submarine that carried twenty-four nuclear warheads they could launch from the middle of the ocean and put on the 50-yard line of Memorial Stadium. The team got the point. If nineteen- and twenty-year-olds are entrusted with that level of responsibility, how much more can we be doing?

Jack has countless examples like that, thanks to his time with the SEALS, and it is always a helpful bit of perspective for our players. In 2016 he accepted an assistant coaching position at Midland University in his hometown of Fremont. Jeff Jamrog, the director of operations who first brought him to talk to the football team in 2011, hired him after he became Midland's head coach. Jack remains a vital member of my team within the team.

Sports psychology has been a career-long passion of mine, and you will find a couple of sports psychologists on my team within the team, too. Dr. Larry Widman has been a valuable resource through the years. I began working with him in 2009, when he was hired as a sports psychiatrist for the university. I did not fully understand the hire. I remember saying, "Why do we have sports psychiatrists around here?" The potential for such hires, however, eventually clicked and I quickly asked Larry if he had ever worked with athletic teams. That, of course, is exactly what he did and it was the start of a fruitful partnership. Larry now runs Performance Mountain, a leadership-consulting group, alongside Jack Riggins. Even though he no longer works in the Athletic Department, I continue to rely heavily upon him.

Over the years Larry has worked closely with our team. He is a specialist in teaching athletes how to deal with high-stress situations by controlling their breathing and focusing on positive self-talk. One of his tenets is that athletes need to manage the physical, technical, tactical, and mental aspects of their performance if they are to reach elite status and be ready to handle high-pressure moments. He has had a big impact on our program.

Larry's role with the team has evolved in recent years. Now he most often works directly with me. I have him at all of our home matches and one or two practices a week, just to watch my body language. He knows me well after all these years together and he can tell through observation if I am dealing with my own stress efficiently. He will also give it to me straight and say, "Hey, your body language sucks." People like that are always good candidates for your team within the team.

Brett Haskell has taken over most of the day-to-day interactions with our team. I have found that one of the real keys to maximizing the effectiveness of your team within the team, once you have it, is working to get those individuals as deeply embedded with your program as possible. Jack has been to China with us. Larry spent many years as a regular fixture in the program. Brett, who works with all the athletic programs at Nebraska, has become more deeply embedded in the last few years and it has made a big difference. She now attends our practice once a week, provides us with weekly reports, and occasionally travels with the team. I think that has given her some ownership over our program. She has bought in and she understands the pressures that we deal with because she sees them on a daily basis. Having her around as much as possible also increases the team's trust in her.

Like Larry, Brett is an expert in team building and leadership development. One of the tasks we gave her coming off our championship season in 2015 was to work with strength coach Brian Kmitta to develop an offseason plan that featured new motivational themes each week. The first week's theme was gratitude. We asked our players to call former players to thank them for everything they had done for the program in the past. We asked our players to thank the trainers and support staff for the work they do to make sure we are successful. We were trying to get the team to understand that they need to be thankful for everything they have here because they are incredibly fortunate to have the facilities and support we have at Nebraska.

If you happened to be watching our social media accounts over that summer, it would have been apparent what our team's theme was each week. I will talk more about this when we talk about goal setting, but that sharing of the goal is a big part of things. Brett wanted the players sharing their thoughts on social media, primarily because it is where they "live" now but also because if they are sharing it, it means they are thinking it and talking about it.

Brett has also been a great resource for me on one of the most important decisions a coach or team has to make each year: team captains. After redshirting a sophomore setter in 2014, we named her co-captain for the 2015 team, alongside senior outside hitter Alicia Ostrander. That was a big step for a sophomore. She had only played sixteen matches for us by that point, but she had demonstrated enough growth as a leader and in practice that we felt good about the decision.

We had an even bigger step in store for that player the following season, however. Our 2016 team had three seniors: outside hitter Kadie Rolfzen, middle blocker Amber Rolfzen, and libero Justine Wong-Orantes. All three were among the best players in the country at their respective positions and any of the three would have made natural captains.

I knew going into that season that I wanted the setter as a captain. She had, after all, just been in that role on a team that had won a national championship. But I also thought we needed to include at least one of the seniors in the mix, so I asked Brett which of those seniors should be named the other captain. "Nobody," she said. "That would be a lose-lose situation for you."

Brett understands these discussions. She understands team dynamics. But I was still a little hesitant. "We've got three seniors and none of them are going to be captains?" I thought. It made me a little nervous. But here is where the value of having Brett embedded with the team paid off. She did not just know about team dynamics in a general sense, she knew about the dynamics of this team.

She convinced me that our seniors would be fine with the setter as the lone captain based on what she had learned from working with the players over the previous season. If anything, Brett told me, picking one of the seniors only had the potential to alienate the other two. The setter, however, had everyone's respect already.

We mulled this decision for about six months. I had numerous meetings with my coaches about it and Brett was the only one in the room saying the team would be fine with the setter as the captain. Eventually that is what we did. Brett did some background work with the seniors once the decision was made. I explained the decision to them each individually, and we gave the three seniors important leadership roles in the areas in which they were the most comfortable. It was the right decision and, in retrospect, should not have been much of a surprise. Brett is trained to understand those scenarios. Me? I am a coach. "How do we win?" sums up my training.

Picking assistant coaches is always one of the biggest decisions any coach has to make. Like recruiting, you cannot be wrong on many of those decisions and expect to win big. There are two keys for me when evaluating potential assistants. One is, can I trust this person? And two is, do they believe strongly enough in their unique experience and insight to share it freely?

It does a coach little good to surround himself or herself with coaches that already think the same way. It becomes too easy for things to become stagnant. Even if you are winning, eventually you are going to run up against some challenges. Maybe the scheme you have always run is not as effective as it once was. Maybe the recruiting pitches that used to work are not the pitches that will work right now. There are hundreds of different problems to solve in any season, and if you have a staff that all think the same way about volleyball, recruiting, leadership, or training, you might find yourself ill-prepared to solve them. Part of the reason connections matter in coaching circles is because it helps answer the question of trust. One must be very careful to not choose the people you know instead of the people who will tell you the truth. Your assistants are really the core of your team within the team, so you want that core to be as strong as possible.

I have had a number of former players coach alongside me over the years. Two of my recent staff members, director of operations Lindsay Peterson and assistant coach Dani Busboom Kelly, played for Nebraska. That comes with some advantages. First, I knew how they had been trained. They came in understanding not just how we did things, but why we did things in that way. Second, both Lindsay and Dani have been really valuable mentors for our current players because they have a shared experience. When a freshman is struggling through the circuit for the first time during off-season training,

Lindsay and Dani know what that is like. They have done it. They can share how they got through it. That ability to relate is invaluable.

I have mentioned Lindsay's remarkable reliability previously—she played in all but 2 sets over a four-year career and missed just the one practice when she was helping deliver a cow on her family farm. These experiences made her the prefect choice for our director of operations. That job requires a high level of organization to navigate all of the decisions that need to be made to get a team through a season. One day Lindsay might be working on our travel schedule for the season, the next she might be going over the budget, and the day after that she might be getting to welcome hundreds of girls for a volleyball camp. I knew Lindsay was capable of handling all of that based on having coached her for four years. I also knew it would not come at the expense of outside-the-box thinking. Lindsay is great at that, too.

Prior to the 2016 season she asked me if I had scheduled my annual meeting with Tom Osborne. I have come to rely on those meetings each year, but it was particularly important before that season. We were the defending National Champions and that in itself casts a season in a different light. It presents an entirely different set of challenges and Osborne had been through it, winning a national title in 1994 and then following it up with another in 1995 while coaching what some consider the best college football team ever.

I had met with Osborne that spring, but that was not really the point. Lindsay was not asking simply as a reminder. She was trying to ensure we as a team had gotten the most out of a resource few programs would be fortunate enough to have. When I told her I had already met with Osborne, she set up another meeting with him and had her own set of questions to ask. That is just one example of the value the right staff member can bring to a team.

Dani shares many of the same skills. She was a small-town, multisport athlete from Nebraska with many of the traits that have become great signifiers for us on the recruiting trail. Originally a setter, Dani moved to libero before our 2006 championship season and became one of the best liberos in the Big 12. I obviously knew Dani the player quite well, but Dani the coach is one of the best I have been around.

She is in tune with young people like no one else. In our program she frequently identified potential problems on our team—personality conflicts, off-the-court disagreements, gaps in leadership—before I even saw them coming. In recruiting she proved her worth over and over with how she related to athletes that we now have to contact very early in their high school careers. Prior to joining my staff Dani spent time as an assistant at Tennessee and Louisville, and her connections there helped us open up new recruiting grounds.

Those connections, in combination with Dani's great success as an assistant, also earned her the head-coaching job at Louisville following the 2016 season. I considered a number of replacements for Dani, but mentally kept going back to former Nebraska players and chose Kayla Banwarth.

Kayla has sort of a classic Nebraska success story. She also was a small-town girl from Dubuque, Iowa, who walked on to the program in 2007 and midway through her true-freshman season had earned the starting libero job. Our history with assistants has shown those two traits—history with the program, small-town upbringing—are pretty valuable. Her success as a Husker, however, was just the beginning for Kayla. She came out of nowhere to earn the starting libero job for the U.S. National Team too, playing on teams that won the 2015 FIVB World Championship and a bronze medal at the 2016 Olympics in Brazil. She was widely regarded as the best passer on the team and most opponents refused to serve to her.

That playing experience was what excited me most about Kayla. She was a great player at Nebraska, she worked hard, and her teammates liked her. I also knew what it took just to be an Olympian, much less succeed as one. Together these certainly outweighed the one thing she lacked: coaching experience. Kayla graduated from Nebraska in 2010, making her a relatively young assistant. But there was little doubt how much coaching meant to her. She told me during our interview that it was her calling, and, while that can be the sort of thing a person just says in an interview, Kayla was showing it, too.

In the spring leading up to the 2016 Olympics, Kayla chose to stay in Anaheim, California, to train. Unlike most of her teammates, she did not have an overseas professional contract. It is hard for liberos to get those jobs, so, as she had done the previous year, she devoted her time to training with Karch Kiraly, the coach of the U.S. National Team, that winter. Training for the Olympics can be a full-time job, but Kayla, having done it the year before, decided she wanted more volleyball in her life. So she took on another job, as a volunteer coach with the Pepperdine University men's volleyball team. It meant that for the entire spring semester of 2016, Kayla got up at 4:30 a.m., drove 55 miles from Anaheim to Malibu—in Los Angeles traffic, no less—helped with practice, then drove back to Anaheim to lift and train. I knew that was how hard Kayla had worked as a player, but it told me a lot about how hard she was willing to work in the next phase of her life as well.

One of the coaches I have always studied very closely is Duke men's basketball coach Mike Krzyzewski. If you look at his bench over the years, it almost always includes former players, so it felt a little bit like fate when in one of my rare moments of channel flipping I stopped on the Duke Basketball Show in December of 2016. Kayla had already agreed to take the job, but it had not been announced yet. I turned on the show and the first coach I saw speaking was Jon Scheyer, a former All-American player at Duke who is now one of Krzyzewski's assistants. Scheyer graduated in 2010, the same year Kayla graduated from Nebraska. It was a nice bit of confirmation that it is okay to hire young assistants, particularly when you know the level of training they received.

In addition to our Nebraska-lifers, we also went out and plucked a couple of the best volleyball minds we could find. Husband and wife Chris and Jen Tamas both serve on our staff, Chris as an assistant and Jen as a volunteer assistant. Part of the thinking with adding them to the team was to really expand our circle of ideas.

Chris was a four-year starter at Pacific and a First Team All-American during his senior year. From there he went on to play for the U.S. National Team and I knew he had learned under some of the best coaches in the country. After his playing career was over, he started his coaching career at California-Riverside, a program that was in the middle of a rebuild. He did well enough there to get a job at Minnesota, one of the Big 10's best programs, and then he jumped right back into a rebuild again at Cal Poly. That told me a lot about Chris right from the start. Those situations are never easy to deal with, but they are the situations when you really learn how to coach. He is a defense-first coach, which meshes with one of my core beliefs about volleyball, but his breadth of experience brought new ideas to the table.

Jen introduced yet another element to the staff. She, too, was a great player at Pacific, earning All-America honors all four years as a middle blocker. She made sixty appearances for the U.S. National Team over eight years and served as captain for four, winning silver at the 2008 Beijing Olympics. In addition to her international experience, Jen also played professionally around the world. One of the biggest things we sell to recruits is that volleyball does not have to stop after college. Thirteen former Huskers have played for the U.S. National Team and many more have gone on to successful professional careers. If a recruit chooses Nebraska and aspires to a professional career, we have a coach on staff who has lived it. Jen knows what it takes to get there.

It helps as a head coach to have a broad circle of mentors and influences. I certainly have that when you look at people like Terry Pettit and Tom Osborne, two of the best in their respective sports. People like Pete Egoscue, Ron Hruska, and Boyd Epley have greatly influenced my approach to training. My broader circle is probably even big enough to include coaches I have never met, because I am constantly reading leadership and coaching books, looking for new ideas and new solutions to the common problems every coach encounters. I am excited and willing to hear just about anyone speak on leadership and motivation. As a coach you have to be that way: open to the wisdom of others and always willing to receive it and see what it can do for you.

You also have to be certain that you have instilled the same passion for ideas in the people you have handpicked to be around you each and every day. This is your team within the team and the people you are going to lean on most often, the people you trust to stay until the job is done, and, most important of all, the people you trust to help young athletes reach their potential. You owe it to your players to make that team within the team as strong as it possibly can be.

Do not create an echo chamber. Do not surround yourself with your buddies. You are looking for people that know sports, know about relationships through experience, know about behavior through observation, and are great at their craft.

My current team within the team includes a former SEALs commander who understands young people and teamwork at a level that was attained in some of the most trying situations anyone will ever experience, period. I have sports psychologists who have devoted their lives to understanding motivation and team dynamics. I have staffers and assistants who all bring unique experiences and strengths to the team. It is a diverse group united by a common goal: What do we need to do to get a little bit better today? The people who will answer that question with "Whatever we can" are the people you want closest to you each day.

Do not look for the people that will tell you what you want to hear. Anyone can do that. It costs nothing and offers just as much. Look for the people who will tell you what you need to hear. That is your team within the team.

1. My early days at Francis Parker School involved coaching a little bit of everything, including middle school boys basketball. Volleyball stuck, however, and in 1986 Francis Parker became the first school from San Diego to win a girls' state volleyball title. (Cook family album)

2. Posing for a photo in front of Saint Basil's Cathedral on a trip to Russia with the U.S. Men's National Team. Early trips abroad instilled in me just how valuable a team-building experience such trips can be. In 1996 Wisconsin became the first college team to travel to Russia. In 2000 Nebraska became the first college team to travel to China. (Cook family album)

3. (*above*) Decked out in my Olympic opening ceremony garb alongside
Lori Endicott, a former setter for the Huskers and member of the 1992 U.S.
Women's National Team. That gave Nebraska two volleyball representatives
in the 1992 Olympics in Barcelona. (Cook family album)

4. Tuna fishing with Taylor off the coast of San Diego. "T-Man" taught me a valuable coaching lesson later in my career and continues to inspire Wendy and me to this day. (Cook family album)

5. Some of my best coaching ideas have come during long walks with Wendy and "the wolfies," our pair of Irish Wolfhounds, Callie and Keaohdan. (Cook family album)

Lt Kevin Davis · Coach John Cook

6. (*opposite top*) Checking an item off my Dream Big bucket list by
going up with the Blue Angels in 2006. We swept Iowa State later
that night. A few years after that flight I earned my pilot's license,
fulfilling a lifelong dream. (Cook family album)

7. (*opposite bottom*) Sharing a moment with Lauren and Wendy after Lauren's
senior-night match against Northwestern at the Coliseum in 2012. My one
regret with Lauren was that I did not recruit her harder out of high school, but,
after a year playing for UCLA, she ended up back home at Nebraska.
(Scott Bruhn, Nebraska Athletic Department)

8. Celebrating with the team after sweeping Texas to take home the 2015 national title. (Aaron Babcock)

9. (*opposite top*) Prehab is not just for players, as I take part in some of the unique exercises and stretches we have honed at Nebraska with the help of Pete Egoscue and Ron Hruska. The exercises are meant to help prevent injuries and put athletes' bodies back into functional positions so they can perform at an elite level. (Aaron Babcock)

10. (*opposite bottom*) Getting a prematch lift in before facing Indiana in Lincoln, Nebraska, in 2016. Strength and conditioning was a passion of mine from my earliest days as a coach, and it continues to this day. (Aaron Babcock)

11. I grew up in San Diego, across the bay from the Navy SEALs' training center; the elite unit has served as a model for our team-building efforts. Here I "debrief" our team, something that happens after each match and practice at Nebraska. (Aaron Babcock)

12. (*opposite top*) Our 2016 senior class had been National Champions before but never Big Ten Champions. We made winning the conference one of our top goals in 2016. The Big Ten race went down to the final day of the regular season, but we won the conference title with a 3–1 win over Michigan in Lincoln. Another goal crossed off our list. (Aaron Babcock)

13. (*opposite bottom*) Another sold-out crowd at the Bob Devaney Sports Center ahead of our 2016 NCAA regional semifinal win over Penn State in Lincoln. Nebraska's nation-leading sellout streak began in 2001, and by the end of the 2016 season had reached 219 consecutive matches. (Aaron Babcock)

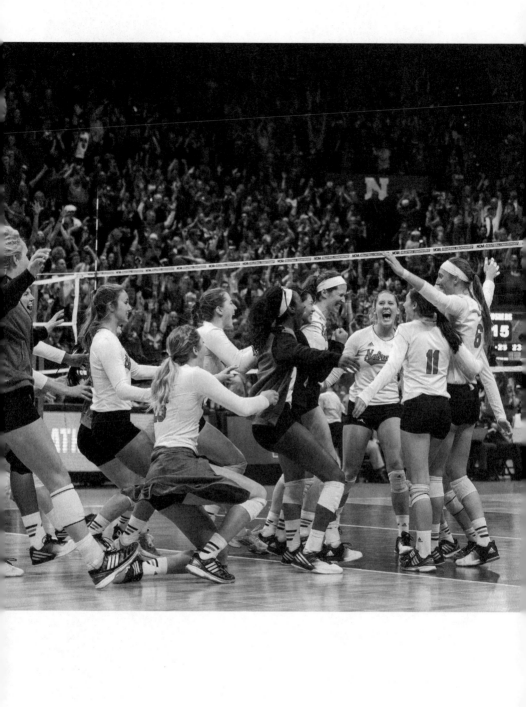

14. The team rushes the floor to celebrate after beating Penn State in five in the 2016 NCAA regional semifinal. The Nittany Lions took the first 2 sets and had a 24–22 lead in the third before we engineered a comeback in one of the most memorable matches of my career. (Aaron Babcock)

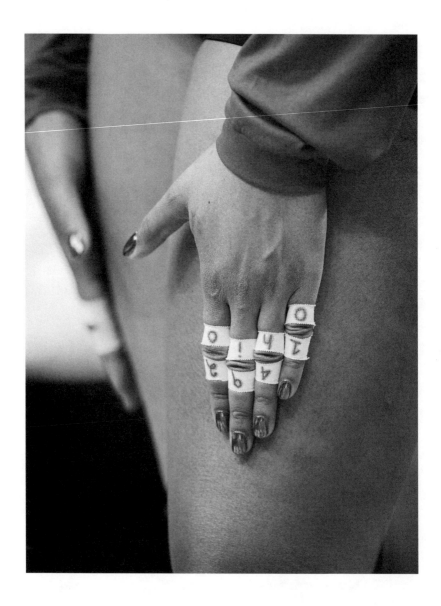

15. The tape on a player's hands prior to our NCAA semifinal matchup against Texas in 2016 in Columbus, Ohio, displayed the number 1492, which was one of our mantras for the season. We used that number to represent our goal of getting back to the Final Four and defending our national title. It became a powerful example of "See it, share it, wear it." (Aaron Babcock)

7

Motivation, Mentors, and a Magician

"There's no such thing as a half-hearted
Kamikaze."—TIM ELMORE, author

The reasons for getting into coaching are often obvious. I have never
met a coach who lasted for any length of time who did not have a
passion for mentoring young people, a love for sport, and a bedrock
belief in the value of athletics as a vehicle for personal growth. Those
are all admirable aims, but if you coach long enough those ideals will
be challenged.

Eventually you will run up against a player you either cannot or did
not reach. You will occasionally drive yourself crazy reliving losses
and failing to appreciate wins. There will be times when the thing you
chose to devote a significant portion of your life to will make you miserable. You will wonder if it is worth it. Doubt will creep in. It happens
to almost anyone who really cares about what they do.

I have gotten through times like those in my own career by thinking
back to the people who mentored me as a young man and the difference they had on my life and career. It was a tactic I learned the day
I almost died on a mountain near Lake Tahoe.

It was July 22, 1980. I was twenty-four years old, just out of college,
coaching football, and playing beach volleyball in my free time. Wendy
and I had been dating for about month and we were scheduled to
play in a beach volleyball tournament in South Lake Tahoe with my
brother, Dave, and his girlfriend, Vicky. We loaded up a Volkswagen
Beetle and drove up from San Diego for the weekend.

After the tournament was over, we stayed over until Monday to do some hiking. The area was in the middle of a heat wave. The Nevada side of the lake saw temperatures as high as 103 degrees, a high the area had not hit since the 1930s. We were on the south side of the lake, where it was no cooler, and headed into what is known as Desolation Wilderness. It has been federally protected land and left primitive since 1931, so this is rocky terrain with no concessions made to hikers. We were not prepared for what we were about to get into.

We parked our car in the morning and hiked 3 or 4 miles into Desolation Wilderness. We spent most of the day trekking over rough granite and climbing over boulders, but we decided to push on longer than we had planned and take in Cascade Falls. We started to make our way there late in the day.

It was closing in on 6:00 or 7:00 p.m. when we reached the top of the falls. We stopped to have some cheese and crackers—the only real food we had brought with us—and prepared for the hike down and around Cascade Lake and back to our car. While we were up above the falls, Dave and I noticed the place was littered with small, loose boulders. Being young and a little obnoxious, we decide to start rolling them off the cliff, watching them fall more than 100 feet straight down and explode on the rocks below. If small boulders made such a satisfying splat, what happens if you try it with a slightly larger one? There happened to be one near the cliff's edge, so I bent down to try and wrestle it from the soil. It did not budge after a few seconds, so I gave up, but when I stood I instantly became light headed and fell backward straight off the falls. In a normal world that should have been it for me, but some mind-blowing things happened once I reached bottom.

I do not remember the fall, but I remember realizing I was hanging upside down in a bush atop some rocks at the bottom of the falls. Wendy, Vicky, and Dave were still all up top, peering over the cliff and assuming the worst. Dave, in what he still maintains is the greatest athletic feat of his life, somehow bounded down the mountain to me where, according to his recollection, I was calling his name. When he arrived I gave him my personal analysis of my situation.

"I think something happened to my hip and I think I knocked some teeth loose," I said.

In reality I had broken my jaw and suffered a compound fracture of my left femur, which was sticking out near my hip. Back at the top of the falls, Wendy and Vicky did not know the extent of anything—only that Dave and I were down at the bottom. They started screaming my name over and over again, hopeful that I would just get up and climb back up the falls. This is when I start to get really lucky.

A hiker coming out of Desolation Wilderness heard the shouting. His name happened to be John, so he thought Wendy and Vicky were calling for him. He also happened to be a respiratory therapist at South Lake Tahoe Hospital. A medical professional! Wendy and Vicky told him what had happened and the three of them started the trek down toward us.

Once they arrived, John assessed the situation and told Dave he was concerned about blood loss. Dave took off his shirt and they applied a pressure pack to my hip. This was mountain territory and it was getting dark, so the hottest day in decades had dipped into the fifties. They built a fire and John told Wendy to go get help. She took off running.

It was a 45-minute hike around Cascade Lake and back to the car. The only shortcut was through the lake and that was when Wendy noticed a man fishing on the lake. She called out to him. "We need help!"

When the man pulled his boat on shore, he told Wendy he was a local sheriff. He radioed for help and then followed Wendy back into the woods and up the mountain to us. I will never forget when he arrived. The sheriff got in my face and asked me what had happened, where am I hurt? It is one of those strange details that sticks with you in a moment of crisis, but his breath smelled like whiskey. Until that point he had been off duty, enjoying a night of fishing. He quickly took control of the situation, however. "You cannot go to sleep," he told me. "You've got to stay awake. We've got help coming."

Three hours later, help finally arrived. The twenty-four-man rescue crew had to hike all the way in and up the mountain. They considered an air rescue with a helicopter but the terrain was too steep to try it, so we waited. Dave had been cradling me for most of the past four hours and he was starting to cramp up. Every time he moved, I screamed out in pain. The situation was pretty hairy at that point.

When the rescue team reached us the EMTs radioed back to the hospital and started asking me the same questions John and the sheriff put me through. Where do you hurt? Did you suffer any head injuries? Once they determined that my jaw was broken, that ruled out any pain medication. I was going to have to tough out the trip down the mountain.

The EMTs strapped me onto a mountain-rescue stretcher, which is really more of a metal basket, and essentially passed me down the mountain. The pain was extraordinary and at that moment I thought of James Rank, my coach at Hilltop High School. He was a hell of a coach and certainly old school. I remembered two moments on that trip down the hill.

One time we were running the Oklahoma drill and I was getting my butt kicked. Next thing I know, I saw Coach Rank headed towards me at a sprint out of the corner of my eye. Not long after that I was on the ground with him on top of me. He had launched into a full-on tackle and once he had me down he got in my face and yelled, "You have got to get tougher, I need you to do this!"

I also thought of the hill behind our practice field. It was steep and Coach Rank made us run it over and over again as a way to weed out those who were not willing to put in the work. For those that stuck it out, he gathered us all around and told us, "You can endure anything." Those were the words I remembered in a life-or-death situation.

There were still no shortcuts around Cascade Lake when we finally reached the bottom, so the team loaded me into the sheriff's fourteen-foot aluminum boat. We were not out of the woods yet.

"We're going to drive across this lake," I remember the sheriff saying. "If we hit a rock and tip over, you're in a metal stretcher and you're going right to the bottom. Are you sure you want to do this?"

I was barely hanging on at that point, but I said, "We've got to do it."

We made it across the lake without issue, where an ambulance was waiting. I was off to the hospital, but I was not done being lucky yet.

The doctor on call the night of my accident was a man by the name of Richard Steadman. If you are a sports fan you have probably read his name a number of times in the newspaper without even realizing it. Over the course of his career, hundreds of world-class professional athletes have gone to Dr. Steadman for their surgeries with potentially millions of dollars on the line. In the mid-1970s, he was sort of a pioneer in the field of physical therapy, leading him to become the team doctor for the U.S. ski team and volunteering his time at the nearby Squaw Creek Olympic training center. An article in the January 1980 issue of *Skiing* magazine called him the "Tahoe magician" for his ability to get athletes back on their feet.

But on July 22, 1980, he was just the surgeon on call at a South Lake Tahoe hospital and I had a pretty serious leg injury that needed attention. Dr. Steadman recognized the gravity of the situation right away, grabbing me by the shirt and pulling himself down close to my face. "You have a compound fracture and an open wound in your leg," he said. "I am going to put you in traction and I have to clean this thing out. It is really going to hurt." They had three nurses hold me down and then used a hose to rinse out the wound. I passed out at that point.

I woke up the next day to find they had drilled a hole through my shinbone, threaded a metal rod through it, and attached weights to the rod to pull me into traction. My jaw was wired shut and the cup of Jell-O and milk on the table beside my bed was an indication of the painful weeks to come.

About a week after the accident, Dr. Steadman came by to see me. We talked about how tough this recovery was going to be and then he told me that he had played football for Bear Bryant at Texas A&M, just a few years after the infamous Junction Boys days. Talk about a guy who could teach you about being mentally tough, Dr. Steadman had some stories about his days in College Station and, as a football coach at the time, it was another one of those little moments during a dark time that made a big difference.

After three weeks in a hospital bed, I was ready to do just about anything to get out. Dr. Steadman visited again and gave me the news I did not want to hear. "John, I am going to leave you in traction because your leg is starting to heal," he said. "I could pin and plate it, but you'll never play sports again. I don't know if you would even walk again."

I thought I was going to lose my mind and Dr. Steadman could see it on my face. He also knew just what I needed at that point. He arranged for Pete Patterson to come visit me.

Pete, one of Dr. Steadman's patients, was an Olympic skier who had just about the worst injury luck you will find with an athlete. In 1971 he broke his back during a downhill run at Junior Nationals. He was back by 1973 but then broke both bones in his lower leg during a competition in Aspen, Colorado. Those bones healed, only for Pete to break them again playing soccer. He was healthy enough to compete in the 1976 Olympics, but broke his femur two years later at the U.S. Nationals in Lake Placid, New York. He recovered from that injury while staying at Dr. Steadman's house and was back in time for the 1980 Olympics where he finished fifth in the downhill, the best finish for an American male in the event at the time.

His message to me was pretty simple: I have been where you are right now. You can do it.

It was what I needed to hear, because after that visit I felt like I actually could come back from this. Pete showed me the things that had helped him when he was laid up for weeks at a time. He made sure I had music and books to keep my spirits high. He also left me with a set of dumbbells. "What am I going to do with those?" I asked.

"You're going to do curls and bench press right here in your bed," Pete said.

"Seriously?"

Having been through long periods of recovery, Pete knew the value of any sort of workout for an athlete, not just in terms of physical strength but mental strength as well. He told the nurses to keep upping the ante on me, and each week they brought in a heavier set of dumbbells. I slowly started making progress and those bed workouts were a big, big part of it.

My mother moved to South Lake Tahoe to help take care of me during my hospital stay. Food processors were still fairly new on the consumer market at that point, but my mom got one and took over the nutrition side of things, grinding up meals and throwing in some vitamins while she was at it. I ended up only losing twenty pounds during my time in bed.

After nine weeks, I was finally ready to be released from the hospital. I still had a full cast on my leg, but one of Dr. Steadman's trademarks was aggressive rehabilitation. He had found that repaired bones heal better if they are stressed within certain limits, so he did not have a problem cutting my cast at the knee, which allowed me to walk. I moved back to San Diego and began my climb back that way.

The first day I was back home, I went out to South Mission Beach and walked fifty yards in the soft sand. The next day, I tried to go seventy-five yards. Three months after being released, the cast finally came off. A year after the accident, I was doing six-mile runs through the sand.

There was some symmetry in that. Part of the reason I was able to recover from the fall at all was because I had been in phenomenal shape at the time of the accident from playing beach volleyball. It was fitting then that the beach was once again what helped bring me back.

This was an experience that really molded me as a young coach and you could say that athletics were there every step of the way. The physical benefits of being an athlete were part of it. The mental strength I learned from a coach was there at a key moment. Dr. Steadman surviving a Bear Bryant practice in the August heat of East Texas pushed him to really expect a lot out of the patients he saw, the people who had no choice but to ask more of themselves than they ever had before; his belief that it was possible had to come from somewhere. Pete Patterson could have quit after any of his numerous injuries, but he pushed through, too, and was there at just the right time to help me do it.

It was easy to feel sorry for myself when I was in the hospital. I had the usual feelings of "How could this happen?" but I was also dealing with some guilt of "How could I be so stupid?" While I certainly would not encourage anyone to spend nine weeks in a full cast if they can avoid it, hospitals are great at changing your perspective.

One of my roommates during that hospital stay was a guy who had been in a motorcycle crash. His leg was basically pinned back together, and he had gangrene. It felt like every day they would come in and have to take another part of his leg and I could hear it happen. It was hard to feel sorry for myself after that. There is always someone who is worse off than you are.

Another one of my roommates was a rock climber. He came in to get arthroscopic knee surgery from Dr. Steadman and spent a few days recovering next to me. I told him my story and, in one of the lighthearted moments, told him I was mad that I had lost my hat. It was a Herman Joseph hat, which was a new beer from Coors brewing at the time. Everyone wanted a Herman Joseph hat.

I would find out later that one of the reasons I survived the 100-foot fall was that there was a two-foot ledge I hit on my way down and it broke my fall. The rock climber was out of the hospital long before I was and one day, eight weeks after the accident, he climbed back up to the ledge and found my hat still sitting there. He brought it to me in the hospital.

The point of telling this story is that sometimes my players tell me I am really tough on them. Sometimes they are right, but it is always with their best interests in mind. I ask a lot of them because I know at some point life is going to ask something much more difficult of them or of someone they love. That is the proper perspective for athletics. Sports are valuable, but they are a diversion.

The hope, however, is that all of those simulated hardships—the tough practices, the offseason conditioning that seems too hard to complete, the sacrifices any great athlete has to make to be the best at a game—show up when the real hardships arrive. Running up a hill as a high school football player may have saved my life when I fell down a mountain.

Every coach has at least one of those moments in his or her past, and every coach is providing similar moments for the young people he leads onto the field or court each day. Remember that the next time the job gets you down.

8

The Longer I Coach, the Less I Know

"With profound success, your head either grows or
swells."—DOUG RATH, Co-Chairman, Talent Plus

In the summer of 2009 I thought I was done with coaching. Following
a camp that June I felt like my world was upside down. I have always
stayed in shape and I know my body pretty well, so I could tell something was off. I told Wendy that I needed to go to the hospital.

At the hospital they put me through a battery of tests but did not
find anything wrong. After a few days I still did not feel right so I went
to the Mayo Clinic in Rochester, Minnesota, for a second opinion.
No physical ailment turned up there either. But the doctors recommended I look into cognitive behavioral therapy. The message they
were essentially conveying was: You have made yourself sick with
the pursuit of perfection.

In many ways the pressure that finally pushed me to the edge that
year had been building up over my entire career. When I arrived at
Nebraska in 1988 it was one of the top programs in the country and
then we went to two Final Fours in my first three years in Lincoln. After
that I joined the men's Olympic team and we won a bronze medal in
1992. It was not until I got to Wisconsin and had my first college head
coaching job that I got knocked down a couple of rungs.

We got hammered that first season in Madison. I had never coached
a losing team and that first year was humbling. It was also instructive.
I learned more about coaching in those first five years at Wisconsin
than at any other point in my career because suddenly I had to figure

things out. I had to build the kind of culture I had experienced both at Nebraska and with the national team. I had to come up with creative ways to build a program.

Eventually we built a winner there and then I was back at Nebraska, where my first team went undefeated and won the national title. At that point I thought I was the best coach in the country. I thought we were going to win the national title every year and I thought it would be easy.

Coaching championship-level teams, of course, is not easy, but once a coach starts down the path of thinking that it is, all the evidence confirming just how hard this job can be becomes even heavier and harder to handle. Our 2001 team was two wins away from the title. The 2002 team was three wins away. The 2003 team lost five games, then we went a combined 63-4 in 2004 and 2005, before finally winning it all again in 2006.

My meltdown in the summer of 2009 was probably most directly a reaction to 2008, and what I felt was a magical season. Part of the reason I held that season in such high regard was because the 2007 season had been so difficult. We imploded at the end of that year and the contrast between those two seasons eventually became too much for me to handle on my own.

The 2007 Nebraska volleyball team was potentially one of the greatest teams ever. We were the defending National Champions and returned four All-Americans from 2006. As a junior in 2006, right-side hitter Sarah Pavan was a First Team All-American, the AVCA National Player of the Year, and the Broderick Cup winner, which is presented to the top female college athlete across all sports. Outside hitter Jordan Larson returned as a junior and was another First Team All-American. Tracy Stalls, middle blocker, was a Second Team All-American and back for her senior season. Setter Rachel Holloway had earned Third Team All-American honors as a freshman the previous season. That team also included Kayla Banwarth, a freshman libero, meaning it had three players, including Sarah and Jordan, who later competed in the 2016 Olympics. The team was absolutely loaded.

It was also a team that never fully came together. I still remember taking our spring break trip to San Diego. We were sitting on the beach after a morning of training and I noticed that Sarah and Rachel had separated themselves and were off on their own while the rest of the team was gathered in one spot. It was apparent to anyone that factions and cliques were forming on the team and I knew immediately that it could derail us. We tried to address it all summer. We talked to the captains. Sometimes, however, there is only so much a coach can control. Sometimes you are not as powerful as the fourteen players on the team.

Still, with that much talent, a team is going to win some matches. We were the preseason No. 1 and held that ranking through the end of October when we finally lost our first match on the road, to No. 5 Texas. We dropped to No. 2 in the country for the remainder of the season but bounced back with eleven straight wins, which put us in the regional final in Madison, against No. 6 California. The Golden Bears swept the match in what had once been my hometown for seven seasons and against the most talented group of players I had ever coached. We did not make the Final Four.

I put a lot of pressure on that team to win it all and the team put a lot of pressure on itself to do the same. At the end of the season I realized I had not done a good enough job. It felt like a wasted year. But the disappointment of that season was not over after the last match.

In February of 2008, after Sarah had become just the fourth player in NCAA history to be named a First Team All-American four times, *Redwire*, a student news magazine produced by the UNL College of Journalism, published a story in which Sarah revealed that while she was at Nebraska she never felt understood and she felt cut off from her teammates. It was a bombshell story, in both local and national volleyball circles. Everyone viewed it as an explanation for why the 2007 team did not bring home a title and suddenly everyone was asking what was wrong with Nebraska volleyball.

Sarah graduated that spring and Rachel, her best friend on the team, gave up volleyball and transferred to Alabama. With Tracy's graduation, our 2008 team only had one returning All-American and we were without our starting setter from the previous two seasons. Our preseason ranking, No. 7, was the lowest at Nebraska in five years and expectations, relative to where the program had been, were pretty low. Even I went into that season thinking "Whatever happens, great," because I did not think we were going to be that good.

I was proved wrong on opening weekend. We started that season in the AVCA Showcase in Omaha. We swept second-ranked Stanford in the first match of the season, then beat fourth-ranked USC in the second. By Labor Day of 2008, the final day of the tournament, we were up to No. 2 in the country and stayed there through October after starting 20-0. We only lost two matches during the regular season, at Colorado and at Texas, and cruised through our first 3 matches in the NCAA Tournament; the first game pitted us against fifth-ranked Washington on its home court in Seattle.

The Huskies crushed us in the first set, 25-14, as we committed 13 errors. Then they won the second, 25-23. Facing elimination, we got a heroic effort out of Tara Mueller, which was pretty emblematic of what that 2008 team had become.

Tara was a backup libero as a freshman in 2007, and, although she had been a highly touted player coming out of high school, nobody knew a lot about her. She won a starting spot on that team and proved more than capable of making teams pay for focusing on Jordan. Tara led with 9 kills in the second set against Washington and again with 8 in the third set as we fought off elimination. Her early contributions in the match were just enough to allow some of our stars to take over. Kayla won the fourth set point on an amazing ace serve and the score at 25-24. We trailed in the fifth set 9-3 before Kayla ripped off 8 straight points from the service line. We took a 14-13 lead before Jordan came up with her own ace. Those were two of the biggest serves in Nebraska history, during the program's first regional win on an opponent's home court. But it was Tara who was named the Most Outstanding Player of the regional tournament. She had already earned First Team All Conference and Second Team All-America honors. It was the best year of her career in a year we needed it most.

The win over Washington sent us back to Omaha to face top-ranked Penn State in the NCAA Championship semifinals. The Nittany Lions, defending champions from 2007 with six All-Americans on the team, were not just undefeated; they had not lost a single set all season. Early on it did not look like we would be the first team to take a set off Penn State.

The Nittany Lions made pretty quick work of us in the first two sets, winning 25–17 and 25–18, their 110th and 111th consecutive sets won. Powered by an NCAA-record crowd in our home state, we had leads in both sets but were not able to hang on. In the third we finally did hang on to an early lead, winning 25–15. The fourth set was back and forth before a pair of kills from Jordan gave us a 25–22 win. That set up a monster fifth set in front of a raucous home crowd.

As most champions have to do at some point, Penn State proved it was capable of handling adversity. We took a 10–8 lead late and the arena was thundering. Following a time-out, Penn State ripped off 6 straight points on its way to a 15–11 win. It was the first time we had lost a match in the state of Nebraska since 2003, but, considering how I thought that season might go, it still felt like a magical ride of a season. When Penn State swept Stanford in the title game, it left our squad as the only team to take a set (two, actually) from the back-to-back champion.

That season should have been a career highlight. We coached, the players played, an incredibly tight team formed, and we achieved more than almost anyone thought was possible. That season is a career highlight now, even though it did not include a national title. At the time, though, it may have been too big of a swing from the season before for me to handle it. Like jumping into a cool body of water on a blisteringly hot day, it felt good but was a shock to the system.

It sort of sent me into a malaise that eventually led to the hospital visits and therapy. The ride had been so improbable and validating that, as the off-season rolled around, I reached a point where I thought, "What else can we do?" We had just played in one of the greatest matches ever in front of the biggest college volleyball crowd to date. I did not think it would ever get any better than that, despite the fact that we had lost.

What I eventually realized was that the solution to the conflict of purpose I was experiencing was visible right there in the 2008 season. It was a season not defined by a championship, but by the journey to get there and the growth that team displayed.

Once you start having success as a coach, you feel like you have to keep proving yourself all the time. If you have achieved *this*, what are you going to achieve *next*? Coaches always feel that way when they are young. We went entire seasons in the Big 12 when we never lost a conference match. That inevitably led me to ask, "What happens when we do?" Eventually it happens, and you start to question yourself. Can I still coach? What could I do better? You tighten up. You press harder. Your team gets tighter. Nobody is having any fun.

This is what eats at coaches. What do you do when all the joy is removed from the thing you love the most? For most young coaches the goal often seems pretty simple: climb to the top, win titles, prove your mettle. Once you have achieved some of those things, however, where do you go? Success suddenly becomes very narrowly defined.

In that summer of 2009 I started to realize I could not continue down that path. I was never going to last. So I took my ego out of it. I recognized that I did not know everything and it was then that I really started to tear down the walls I had built around myself as a coach. I went back to my "team within the team" and started to rely on the people closest to me for guidance. I opened myself up to the expertise of people outside of that circle, too. I started reading more and more books from coaches. I studied other successful teams. Instead of viewing everyone else's experience as something to be measured against mine, I began to recognize that each person's experience is unique. If you are willing to listen, everyone may have expertise that can help you.

At that point the message became pretty clear: I did not have to prove myself anymore. I was not going to be defined by wins and losses. Instead, my coaching career was going to be centered on enjoying the experience of leading young people and doing the best we could every day. Rather than viewing each season as either a step forward or a step backward—based on what we had done in the past—I was going to embrace that idea that each season and each team is a journey unto itself. That is always true, and it had always been right there for me to see if I had been willing to look.

I finally started to see it when I had to step back to evaluate myself before the 2009 season. Disappointing as the season was, the 2007 team taught me a ton. The 2008 team gave me an entirely different experience. With each team after that, I started to learn more and more. Some of the players I coached after that point—Hannah Werth, Gina Mancuso, Brooke Delano—made me realize there was so much more to learn if I just opened my mind and did not have to pretend I knew it all.

Prior to that point I believed my career would be about compiling experience: stacking the wins, losses, awards, titles, and scars earned over each season. That is the value of experience, right? There is no shortcut to getting experience and it is uniquely yours. One of the key moments in my coaching career came when I realized I was wrong about that. The truth was, the longer I coached the less I knew.

I was twenty years into my college coaching career and had nearly thirty years overall coaching experience when my thinking started to shift. In studying the careers of other coaches and their successes and failures, it seemed like another major theme was emerging: if you remain open-minded, your ego will evaporate with experience. That is the *real* value of experience.

This ego evaporation is a gradual process. Even as I started to embrace these ideas around 2009, I sensed it was going to take a while to be able to fully implement them. I still thought of myself as an old-school football coach and in many ways I still do. It was the culture I had been exposed to as a young athlete. For example, one of my assistant high school football coaches, Wayne Sevier, who went on to become Joe Gibbs's offensive coordinator for eleven years with the Washington Redskins, lived in a camper in the parking lot outside the football stadium. I saw a lot of that classic archetype of the coach who was almost compulsively committed to winning and being the definitive voice on every aspect of the team; the top-down leader. I was that coach for a number of years and it worked well for me.

Changing that approach wouldn't happen immediately. There were times I resisted the new way of thinking and fell back on the old way. I remember in 2010 our team went to Texas. We were 19-1 and ranked No. 2 in the country; Texas was No. 10. ESPNU was carrying the game and analyst Holly McPeak, a beach volleyball Olympian, stopped by the arena to watch our practice before the game. Practice was dreadful.

Our players were so out of it that they could not remember where to line up and I lost it and started screaming in front of the broadcast team. After the practice Holly came up to me and asked if my team was always that out of it and if that was how I always reacted. "No," I said, "but they really upset me today."

Of course we went out and played terribly in the match. Texas took the first 2 sets, we battled back to take the third, and then the Longhorns polished us off in the fourth. The pressure of that big match on national television had clearly gotten to our players, probably because it had clearly gotten to me. I felt it and snapped at practice. The team could see I was uptight and it filtered down to them.

As the years have gone on, however, those sorts of reactions have become more and more uncommon. I will still be tough when a shock is needed, but sometimes, particularly in this day and age, the situation calls for calm and love.

Early in the 2016 season, after our team had opened the year with huge wins over top-ten teams Florida and Texas to become the unanimous No. 1, we hosted Iowa State and Oregon State for the Nebraska Invite. In the week leading up to the tourney I noticed the players were horsing around a lot. After two huge wins to open the season, the team felt like it had already arrived. Rather than immediately try to knock them down a little bit, I sought the advice of Brett Haskell. "This team thinks they're hot stuff already," I told her.

"So they're really kind of playful?" she asked.

"Yeah."

"The message you need to give them is that it is okay to be playful, but you've still got to be focused," Brett said.

She was right. My response a few years earlier would have been to tell the team they were screwing around too much and they were going to get knocked off. Past players could handle that. Some of them wanted it. But Brett knew this team needed some positive reinforcement along with the criticism. We went out and swept Iowa State.

A day later, Oregon State really brought the fight to us in the first set, jumping out to a 6-1 lead. I thought about taking a time-out, but I decided to let the team play through it. When the first TV break came, I could have gotten in their face, been the old-school football coach, and let them have it.

Instead, I opted for confidence. "Hey, guys, I know it's not real smooth right now, but just keep going point by point," I said. "We'll work our way back into this and we'll start playing better."

We did, rallying to win the first set and sweeping the Beavers. We have a postgame debriefing after each match and that night I asked the players what they had learned. The feedback I received was that the talk during the first time-out made a huge difference. The players acknowledged that they were playing poorly and probably deserved to be told as much. When I did not do that, the team relaxed and was able to play to its potential.

It took me about twenty-five years to get to the point where I was willing to do the right things in that tournament—ask for help from a staff member, resist my initial instinct to micromanage our performance. If you had told me ten years prior to that day that my response in the huddle to going down 6-1 to an unranked team on our home floor would be "We're going to work through this," I would have told you that was impossible. There was no way I was going to take the easy way out and give the team a pass. That possibility would not have even registered with me.

Neither would what I was thinking as the team came to the bench for that time-out. It was not about the game. It was about the bigger picture. "If we get knocked off today, then, you know what, we get knocked off," I was telling myself. "We'll learn from that and we'll move on."

I took my ego out of the equation. Like a lot of coaches it took me a long time to reach that point, but you see it pretty often with leaders as they progress through their careers. I have seen many coaches get emotional when talking about some of their former players or teams and reflecting on the relationships they built and the growth they witnessed. It does not happen when they are talking about big wins or crushing losses.

It happened to me after the season-opening tournament in Oregon at the start of 2016. As defending champs we had dropped our first set of the year to No. 10 Florida but then responded by winning the match in four. The next day, against No. 2 Texas, the school we had beaten nine months earlier to win the 2015 national title, we fired on all cylinders and swept the Longhorns. In the locker room after the match I started to tear up as I talked to the team. To someone outside the program it looked like two impressive wins to start a season. But I was thinking about the eight months of work the players and staff had put in to play that well against two of the top teams in the country. Defending a championship is difficult, but we laid out our plan the previous January, the players stuck to it during spring drills, and then they continued to train at a very high level when they were on their own in the summer. "Unstoppable" had been one of our themes during the off-season and I told the team that those two matches were evidence they had put in the work necessary to be unstoppable. That was one of the top-ten moments in my career.

This is now what I find most rewarding as a coach. It's not the wins themselves. It's what it takes get them. Seeing players make individual breakthroughs, on and off the court, brings me joy. It makes me happy when those players, unprompted, use the language and ideas we have been hammering home in an interview or article. When our team plays with heart and gives everything, win or lose: this is the ultimate satisfaction.

How does a young coach get to that point without having to learn it the hard way? It is not easy. You could start by not walling yourself off from the ideas of others. Developing my team within a team was a huge part of my coaching transformation. Great leadership is not about doing it all yourself. Trust others to see the things you cannot see and rely on their expertise.

Sharpen your focus. Perhaps the best way to avoid being defined by wins and losses is to concentrate on the path to those results. Build your thinking around the day-to-day process. Have a plan, execute it as best you can that day, and then move on. The harder you hold on to perfection and the more stress you create, the more elusive perfection becomes and the harder it will be for your team to perform at its highest level.

If you start to feel worn down by the coaching grind, take stock of your decision-making process. How many of your decisions are driven by ego? How much more do you think you have to learn, and how much are you convinced you already know? It was only after I recognized that I still had a lot to learn that things really changed for the better.

I have three questions I ask myself each day, which have really helped achieve this balance: first, Who needs me today? I borrowed that one from Rhonda Revelle, Nebraska's softball coach for the past twenty-five years. It is how I start each morning. I take stock of what I have noticed from our players and coaches and determine who needs my help the most. Sometimes it is just a note or a text. Other times it is a conversation. But I try to do something each day to pick someone up or give them the motivation they need to help us reach our potential as a team. One of the keys to having a great culture and a great team is keeping a high level of happiness. You want a team that is inspired, that wants to work hard and, most important, that wants to be there. That alone is a big chunk of what it takes to have a successful unit.

Second, Would I be chosen today? If our athletic director were hiring a volleyball coach right now, would I still be the choice? Can you look yourself in the mirror and say you are doing a good enough job that you would be hired again? Am I cutting corners? Do I have regrets? It is a great way to hold yourself accountable and a trick I share with coaches all the time.

Third, Would I want to be coached by me? This is the most important to me. I want to leave the gym each day knowing that our players want to come back the next day to be coached again, to practice again, to play another match, and they want to be led by me. I ask myself if I have done a good enough job coaching, whether being positive or negative, being hard on them or patting them on the back, to the point that they want to come back. If we can do that every day, we will have a team that is enjoying the journey.

9

Destination Omaha

"There is more in us than we know if we could be made to
see it; perhaps, for the rest of our lives we will be unwilling
to settle for less."—KURT HAHN, German educator

Omaha has hosted the NCAA Division I Women's Volleyball Championship tournament three times. First, in 2006, when we won the national title. In 2008 we battled back from two games down against Washington on its home floor just to get to Omaha, then we nearly upset an almost unstoppable Penn State squad. In 2015 we decided to embrace the fact that the championship weekend was returning to our home state and what it meant from the very start.

"We have a great opportunity to get to Omaha and be in a Final Four," I said right at the top of my preseason press conference to open the season. We were ranked fifth in the preseason AVCA poll, so we were definitely in contention. But technically we were not picked to reach the Final Four. Our theme for the season was going to be "Destination Omaha."

You could feel the room full of reporters sort of take a collective breath of surprise. The "Just take it one game at a time" approach is common among coaches across all sports. Do that and nobody raises an eyebrow. That is how coaches are supposed to talk. It signals that seasons are not necessarily defined by winning or losing.

You can even get away with operating at the other end of the spectrum, so long as you keep it pretty general: "Our goal is to win a national championship." That works because it indicates the team believes it is capable of anything and every team should feel that way at the start of the season.

At Nebraska we try to make goal-setting more specific than that, and, in truth, my confident comments about Destination Omaha in that season-opening press conference probably disguised the internal debate on the topic we had been having as a staff. Most people would say you are crazy for laying out such a specific barometer for success in an individual season. We considered that possibility before deciding to move ahead and make it public.

Leading up to the 2015 season, from January to August, all we heard from our fans was that they had already purchased their tickets for the Final Four and that they would see us in Omaha. Every day it was "Omaha." It is good to have that level of belief in the program, but it presented a philosophical question when it came to laying out the goals for the team: Do we embrace this or avoid it? In 2006 and 2008, getting to Omaha and the Final Four was a goal we set with those teams, but we kept it internal. Publicly acknowledging that reaching the city less than hour away was one of our goals in 2015 was another thing entirely. I went to my staff and presented them with the choice of either talking about it or not talking about it. Everyone agreed that we should put it out there and go for it.

We did a number of things to help our 2015 team visualize what it would mean to get to play in front of 17,000 fans, almost all of them pulling for Nebraska. Before spring practice started that season we put up photos of the CenturyLink Center, the Omaha arena hosting the Final Four. We put up a photo of the sign on Interstate 80 just outside of Lincoln, which read that Omaha was only 48 miles away. When we played Creighton in Omaha in September we had our players take selfies in front of the arena. It did not hurt that three of the players on that team were from the Omaha area and 40 percent of the team was from Nebraska. Omaha was a destination they all knew very well.

But the biggest thing we did was get t-shirts. Once we decided that Destination Omaha would be a rallying cry for 2015, we had Kadie Rolfzen, a graphic-design major, design t-shirts featuring what would become our mantra for the season. She designed fifteen different logos and we settled on one that had the state outline of Nebraska along with a star denoting Omaha's location. We printed it on black shirts and started wearing them. As soon as our fans saw the shirts, we started getting calls asking where they could purchase them. Everybody was all in on Destination Omaha from the moment they heard it. All season long the team ended practice with a huddle and Justine Wong-Orantes would say "Destination" the rest of the team responded "Omaha."

Once we started to work our way into the season, I felt very comfortable coaching with the weight of Omaha on our shoulders. I liked how we were preparing early in the year. I could see that we were doing everything we could to get to Omaha, and I knew based on two previous trips there for Final Fours, special things could happen if we made it and had our home crowd behind us. Aiming for the Final Four and a national championship was not really new, of course. We have goals like that every year. But sharing those goals so widely was different. Not really for us, but for everyone else.

At Nebraska, we have made a point to try and take goals beyond something that is simply written on a white board at the start of a season. Our philosophy has been defined by the idea of "See it, share it, wear it," and Destination Omaha was perhaps the most public unveiling of that process.

Athletes are often visual learners, particularly in this day and age. If players can see something, feel it, and touch it, they are much more likely to remember it. If you have watched a college football game recently, you have seen this idea at work. Whether it is a team trying to run an up-tempo offense or a defense trying to combat it, you frequently see assistant coaches on the sidelines holding up placards that feature a seemingly random collection of cartoon characters, celebrity photos, logos, or popular Internet memes. That is how many teams signal plays and formations in a fast-paced game, because it is a lot easier for a player to remember the play associated with a funny photo of Michael Jordan than it is to remember the name of the play itself. If the method didn't work, coaches wouldn't be doing it.

We push that idea to the limit Our seasons are full of slogans and sayings, maybe little scraps of inspiration our coaches or players find along the way, and they can come from anywhere. For the major themes there is always a visual component. It has become something of a trademark for us.

My first real experience of trying to take an idea and make it a tangible goal was late in my first season at Nebraska in 2000. We were 28-0 headed into the NCAA Tournament and I could tell the pressure of that record was starting to weigh on the players. Trying to maintain an undefeated season starts to feel like you are carrying around a thousand-pound boulder. It almost got us in the regular-season finale at Kansas State.

To that point in the 2000 season we had faced a fifth game just one time, beating UCLA in five in early September. That team was also trying to become just the second team in school history to finish the regular season undefeated. We ended up beating No. 22 Kansas State in five, a program we were 61-1 against all-time, but only after going down 2 sets to 1. It was not a fun match and I realized we needed to do something to try and relieve the pressure of being 28-0 before the national tournament started.

It made me think of something I had read in one of Phil Jackson's books. The eleven-time NBA champion coach always used a thoughtful approach to motivation that was heavily influenced by a mix of eastern and Native American spiritualism. The style does not always appeal to everyone, but it is tough to argue with Jackson's results. I thought it was just what that particular team needed.

Before the start of the tournament we bought a Hula hoop and fashioned it into a giant dream catcher. Then we had the team write down their fears on a piece of paper and one by one they attached them to the dream catcher. Once we had everyone's notes posted, we talked about them—and then took all of those scraps and burned them in our team lounge. The last step was totally Jackson's, but I did not have a problem stealing it from him. Coaches have always been great thieves.

Did lighting our fears on fire help us win our final 6 matches and the national title that year? It apparently did not hurt. The larger point, though, was what we always strive for: the players were able to see their fears and share them with their teammates. Once we had all those fears acknowledged and up on the dream catcher, the players could see that many of the same things they were stressing about individually were shared by their teammates. An individual burden became a team burden, and we were able to unite and try to shoulder those burdens together. We burned those fears but kept the dream catcher to catch any other bad stuff that might come through during the tournament. We hauled it with us all the way to the final 2 matches in Richmond, Virginia. We have had numerous examples like that over the years.

In 2011 the Final Four was at the Alamodome in San Antonio. As a staff we always spend a lot of time brainstorming in the spring, trying to come up with the ideas and themes we will use to motivate our team through the off-season. This is another example of when having assistants from a younger generation with a different perspective pays off. As we looked at that season, we thought making San Antonio an internal goal was justified. One of my assistants mentioned that there was a company that could turn any photo into a puzzle. We took a photo of the team, superimposed it onto a picture of the Alamo, and for $19.00 we got a 500-piece puzzle.

Once we had the puzzle, we broke it apart, separated the puzzle pieces into plastic bags of ten pieces each, and spread those bags throughout campus. During the summer leading up to the season we told our players that these puzzle pieces were scattered around campus and that to get them they would have to go and share their goals, both personal and for the team, with people we trusted. Dennis Leblanc, the team's adored academic advisor, had some pieces. Tom Osborne, the athletic director at the time, had some. Coaches of other sports at Nebraska had some. We did not make the 2011 season about "Destination San Antonio," but we shared that goal beyond the confines of our own locker room. We knew the goal of reaching the Final Four would mean more if the players had to tell someone else, someone not really connected to the program, about the thing they wanted the most. Goals are most valuable when they are acknowledged and shared.

We gave that team until August 8, the start of fall camp, to collect all of the pieces of the puzzle. To get all of the pieces, for example, the players would have to schedule a meeting with Bo Pelini, the head football coach at the time, and go tell him about their goals. I still remember my daughter, Lauren, calling me the minute after she had finished her meeting with Pelini. "I am so pumped right now," she told me. "I'm not just ready to go play volleyball. I want to go play football!"

When the team got together for the first practice of the season, we had the players put the puzzle together from the pieces they had collected. Once it was done, we had it laminated and framed, and then it hung in the Coliseum every day after that. We did not end up making it to San Antonio, losing to Kansas State in Lincoln in the second round of the tournament, but the players' response to that goal-setting exercise only furthered my own personal belief in the "See it, share it" philosophy.

We have continued to push that idea as the years have gone on. Our 2012 team all got decks of goal cards. They were not altogether different than the play placards you see in college football these days. For example, it was really important to Gina Mancuso, a senior outside hitter on that team, to be a captain. So, during that summer we gave her a goal card that included an image of Cap'n Crunch. Hayley Thramer, a junior middle blocker, had overcome a shoulder surgery early in her career, so we gave her a goal card that included a photo of Drew Brees, quarterback of the New Orleans Saints. He had overcome a major shoulder surgery to rank among the best quarterbacks in the NFL, so the connection was natural.

We did this for every member of the team and compiled all of these images and put them on laminated cards. We handed out three to each player: one to hang on her backpack, one to put in her locker, and one to take home so she could see it every day. Odds were good that anyone around the players that season saw those strange little cards with a somewhat odd collection of images and asked about them, too. A goal is most powerful when you see it, share it, wear it.

I love to incorporate pop culture into our goals and motivational tactics. I have probably shown clips from *Top Gun* to every team I have ever coached at Nebraska. The aerial scenes in the movie were filmed at Miramar Naval Air Station in San Diego, so the film had a big impact on me personally. It is also something the players like watching and there are some good messages in there. "Never leave your wingman," one of the most famous lines from the movie, is something we use all the time to remind players about how we need to move on the court. If one player rotates to cover a gap or play a ball, no matter if that is the right or wrong decision, everyone else has to rotate with her. Never leave your wingman. Using the movie to highlight that point makes it somewhat fun to remember, and those things have an impact. Angie Oxley, who played on our 2000 team and is now an assistant coach at Creighton, sent me a *Top Gun* t-shirt near the start of the 2016 season. Sixteen years after her playing career had ended, Angie was still thinking about "Never leave your wingman."

I showed our 2015 team the famous clip from the movie *Spartacus* in which the Romans offer to spare the lives of the slaves if they will simply give up Spartacus. In the scene the slaves all rise up one by one to shout "I'm Spartacus," refusing to give up their leader. We used that clip to illustrate how strong a team needs to be. It may have worked too well. For the rest of that season and into 2016, any time I would come in and say something like, "Who left a mess in the locker room?" the team would always respond "Spartacus."

Things like that, the little inside jokes that emerge among friends, become a really fun part of coaching. I always say there is both art and science to coaching, and the art part of it can be really fun. We are constantly trying to think of ways to motivate and inspire a generation that is not used to storytelling. Mixing in movie clips has become a fun but effective way to do that. You never know when something is going to stick with the players and become a meaningful teaching point.

Our 2016 team, which was trying to become the first in school history to win back-to-back national titles, had a number of different motivational themes. One of our shorthand sayings was B2B, for "back-to-back." We also used 1492, because "in 1492 Columbus sailed . . ." You know the rest. The 2016 Final Four was in Columbus, Ohio. Short little things like that work great as daily reminders. Our players' lockers all have mini iPads in them and have constantly rotating images of some of our sayings. We can control remotely what shows up on those screens, so we change those about once a week just to keep things fresh. It is another small detail, but you might be surprised about the impact that a new photo or message has on a Monday morning. The players almost have to stop and think, "Okay, what is the message we should be thinking about?"

"Dream Big" has been a consistent message throughout my career, so when we sat down together as a staff to determine what our goals would be and how we would convey them, we realized that the team was facing a special challenge as defending champs. How do you acknowledge that? Or, do you acknowledge that?

Having just navigated the road to Omaha the season before, there was little hesitation to acknowledge that 2016 was going to be tougher. We had some debates over how to convey the point. We kicked around some ideas until one of my staff members suggested "Dream Bigger." As often happens, the simplest solution was the best. Dream Bigger references one of the key ideas in our program and also conveys the point that the season to come is going to require an even greater effort—more focus, more determination, more sacrifice.

As a reward for winning the national title in 2015, I hosted my assistants and their significant others on a trip to Cabo San Lucas, Mexico. One of our activities was to visit Playa del Amor, also known as Hidden Beach, because it sits under a rock formation that hides it from view. It is a national park and only accessible by boat. We rode out there, walked through the water to the shore, and as soon as we got ashore we saw an old man selling handmade bracelets with the names of American sports teams—Lakers, Cowboys, Yankees—sewn into them.

I asked him if he could put anything on the bracelets. He said he could so I wrote down "Dream Bigger" on a scrap of paper and handed it to him. Ten minutes later I had a bracelet with our team mantra for the season. I then asked the man if he could make twenty-four more. He said he would, but the bracelets would not be ready until the next day. I went back a day later and we left Mexico with enough bracelets for our entire team.

The players and coaches wore them all season long. It was just another small but tactile reminder of what we were after, something that can take on extraordinary meaning. Before we faced Iowa State early in the 2016 season I took off the bracelet to shower and get dressed for the match. We went down and went through our usual pregame routine and it was not until the match was just about ready to start that I realized I was not wearing the bracelet. I had one of our trainers run up to my office in the Devaney Center to get it. No way I was coaching without it. See it, share it, wear it.

In addition to our big motivational themes each season, we have more technical match-to-match and season-long goals, just like most coaching staffs do. While my career has been marked by a lot of change and a willingness to embrace it, one thing that has always remained the same is a defense-first approach. That is how I started my career as a football coach and it has carried straight through to volleyball—defense wins championships, no matter the sport.

You cannot prepare for a great defensive team. But a defensive team can prepare for a great offense and how to stop it. In volleyball, if you are going against a great defense you are going to eventually run out of answers. There is nothing you can do. If a team is expected to dig balls and block balls and pressure with the serve, there is nothing an opponent can really do to prepare.

Philosophically our teams have always been based in serve-block-defense. That is our core. We try to be low error and then be able to win the national championship points—the long rallies, the plays when it gets down to a 2-point set. I tell the team this every year. One of our first goals each season is to be the best defensive team in the conference. Defense is the one thing that you can always hang your hat on because ultimately you can control both how you play defense and your effort and preparation.

What does that look like in practical terms? We have a lot of numbers we try to hit from game to game, which are posted in the notebooks the players always have with them. One set of numbers that I think is ingrained in every match I have ever coached is .300–.150. We want to have a hitting percentage of at least .300 and hold our opponent to .150 or less. Those are admittedly ambitious goals. There are usually only around five Division I teams that are going to hit .300 every season and only five or ten that are going to hold their opponents to .150. The team that can do both is winning a lot of matches. We have done it four times: 2000, 2001, 2002, and 2005.

We have a few other general numbers that apply to every match and every season. We want to score 45 percent of the time when we have the serve and 65 percent of the time when our opponent has the serve. We want to dig 70 percent of the balls hit to us. Beyond that, however, our statistical goals quickly start to get pretty deep and specific.

Our numbers are managed by Natalie Morgan, who joined the program in 2014 as our video coordinator. But she is also our go-to stats person. Natalie played at Oregon State before her career was cut short by injury. Today she runs our Data Volley system, an intense computer program that will give you every number you could ever want if you have someone who can run it. Natalie might code fifty individual events in a rally. It takes serious training to be able to do it, but in our experience it is an investment that is worth it.

Not unlike football coaches, we will go through and grade every play after a match. Blocking, serving, and passing are all scored on a four-point scale. We want to hit efficiency goals in each of those four areas. We also pay close attention to rotation data. A volleyball match is 6 mini games, and if one of your rotations is not performing, you need to figure out a solution. We use the rotation data to structure practices; we have to figure out how to make our weakest rotation better through training.

The deeper down the rabbit hole we go, the less we share with the players on a regular basis. We are not telling a player every day what her dig percentage is, for example, but we visit things like that every so often and everyone knows the numbers we want to hit.

These are stats at a very, very high level, and that is really just the meat and potatoes of it. There is dessert, appetizers, and plenty more, if you want to go get it. Some of the other big-name programs like Penn State and Minnesota have full-time stats people now, but still only about 10 percent of the teams out there do. I like having access to those numbers because I think it gives us an edge. But I do have to be careful that I do not look at them too much. This is the science part of the coaching equation, and I still want to be able to coach with instincts, too. No matter what the numbers say, at some point you are just going to need a player to make a play.

One of my earliest coaching memories is going to a coaches' conference in San Diego where Don Coryell was the featured speaker. Coryell revolutionized passing offense as the head coach at San Diego State before moving to the NFL as a coach with the St. Louis Cardinals and the San Diego Chargers. At the conference, Coryell was talking about an end-game situation during his time with the Chargers. This was back when San Diego had the all-pro quarterback-receiver combo of Dan Fouts and John Jefferson.

As Coryell told it, the Chargers were facing a do-or-die play near the end of a game so he called a time-out to talk it over. There was some disagreement among the coaches about what play to call. They debated for a while and when the time-out was over, nobody seemed to feel great about the play the team was about to run. Just as Fouts was headed back onto the field, Coryell said he grabbed his quarterback and said, "Just throw to J.J." Fouts did, Jefferson caught it, touchdown Chargers.

Stats are great, but that's coaching, too.

Our 2015 road to Omaha took a pretty big detour in the middle of October—big enough that I was not sure we were going to get back on track. The opening two months of the season had gone well enough. We opened the season 16-2, with the two losses coming to third-ranked Texas and thirteenth-ranked Ohio State. We were 7-1 in Big Ten play and tied for the conference lead. That set up two huge back-to-back matches on our home court against ninth-ranked Minnesota, also in a tie for first in the conference, and sixteenth-ranked Wisconsin. These are the weekends that can swing seasons, so we pulled out all the stops.

We honored our 1995 and 2005 teams prior to the match against Minnesota on Friday and the biggest crowd of the season was ready to be loud. Our team was less ready to play, however. The Gophers won the first two sets on their way to a 3–1 win. It was a frustrating match on a number of fronts. We fell a game behind in the standings, but, more than that, the team just was not ready to play. Thinking that we could turn it on when necessary had been an issue for that team to that point in the season, and it finally got us against Minnesota. I left the arena that night thinking we would find out how tough our team was by how it responded with another highly ranked team the next night.

The answer we got was not the one I wanted. We took the first set, but the Badgers dominated us defensively to take the next 3 sets and the match. We made thirty-five attack errors and hit a season-low .133. It was the first time since Nebraska had joined the Big Ten in 2011 that we lost back-to-back matches on our home court. I left the arena that night thinking there was no way we were getting to Omaha.

I am pretty sure no one else on our team was thinking we would at that moment either. We were now thinking, "Let's just get to the NCAA Tournament." But the Monday after those matches, Dani Busboom Kelly met with some of our team leaders at their request. They unburdened themselves a little bit and sort of re-committed to the path we had laid out. We finished the regular season with 10 straight match wins. That was not enough for us to win the Big Ten: the loss to Minnesota left us 1 game behind the Gophers at the end of the season.

It was enough, however, to make Destination Omaha feel like a real possibility again. That is the real key when it comes to setting a goal: you have to know where you want to go. I always tell people, you do not go to the airport to figure out where you are going to fly and then get on a plane. You go there with a destination in mind. However, having a destination, having goals, is often not enough. Successful people use goal-setting as a powerful accomplishment tool, but there are also plenty of people who set goals and then never look at them again. That is why we have made "See it, share it, wear it" such a key part of our program. Players share their goals with past champions at Nebraska or the athletic director and other coaches because it broadens their circle of accountability. If the head football coach knows how high a player's goals are, it means something much different than if the player simply keeps them to herself or within the team itself.

The 2015 Destination Omaha season was perhaps the most visible example of having accountability on goals. There was not a day during that season that someone on our team was not wearing one of the shirts. We saw the message every day and we did not care if everyone else saw it, too. In fact, it is exactly the plan we had put in place. There is gold in having goals, but there might be even more value in sharing their riches before you even know they are yours.

10

Two Points Better

"The harder the conflict, the more glorious the triumph."
—THOMAS PAINE, English American philosopher

Coaching often feels like a series of big decisions made to win big games. Leading a team is a massive undertaking. Every choice and every decision ultimately falls under the coach's discretion, and you can never totally know which one of those decisions may end up making the difference between winning and losing. Every decision matters and the best coaches carefully consider each one. If those decisions end up being good decisions on the whole, your team will probably find itself in some big games. That is when the scope changes.

We make an effort at Nebraska to make the biggest matches feel the smallest. Coaches know when they are facing an equal team. The players know when they are going into a big game; the pressure builds, the outside attention cranks up, and the intensity goes up a notch. Many coaches try to downplay those factors by taking "just the next game on the schedule" approach, but rather than ignore the external factors that come with truly big matches, we we have a method for making it manageable for the players: Be two points better.

Two points better is what you have to be in volleyball to win a game. Do that three times and you have won the match. That means that in total we have to be six points better than our opponents. When we are getting ready to play a Penn State or a Texas or some other college volleyball heavyweight, I guarantee that at some point before the match I will mention that it is just "three games, two points." Plenty of other coaches and leaders have their little mantras. Urban Meyer wrote in his book, *Above the Line*, that one of the pillars of Ohio State's culture is "four to six, A to B." Meyer preaches to his players to go as hard as possible for four to six seconds, the duration of the average football play, and take the most direct route to where their assignment tells them to be, A to B. That is a football spin on the same principle we use. Managers and CEOs can find one that applies to their specific tasks. Coaches can find one that applies to their specific sports. For us, it's "Two points better."

The key to getting something like that to stick is to make it quick, simple, and memorable. The primary goal is having a mantra, not necessarily a lot of theory. You want something your players can repeat to themselves when the game is on the line. You want something they do not have to remember, but rather cannot help but remember. You want it echoing in their heads. If you can do that, you make the game manageable. You are no longer talking about beating the best team in the conference, district, state, or country. You are talking about the things you have to do to beat *any* team. It takes a high-stakes game, the game everyone is talking about, the game with everything on the line, and puts it on the same scale as every other game.

It is hard to go on the road in a regional final and beat one of the best teams in the country on its home floor. But being two points better? That is doable. You have already acknowledged that the match is going to be close. The team is prepared for that. Now it is just a matter of being a little bit better.

Once you have found a mantra that sticks, the application of that mantra is almost limitless. We use "Two points better" in our training when our players are struggling to finish a drill or trying to knock out the last set of the circuit. It is also a big part of how we approach off-the-court decisions that have the potential to affect the team.

Freshmen in particular have a hard time believing what you are telling them early in their careers because they have not seen it work for themselves. But the bottom line is they have to be able to make great decisions all week long. We ask: Do you get up and get to class on time, or stay in bed? Do you make good choices and eat right, or take the easy route and stop at the drive-thru? Do you go to bed at a reasonable hour, or spend another half hour on your phone? Are you making smart decisions when it comes to your social life?

We tell our players that if they are skipping class, skipping meals, staying up too late, or partying too much, they are not making the choices necessary to be two points better. How can a player expect to make great decisions when the score is 23–23 in the third set of a huge match if they have cheated themselves all week? They can't. The player who has made the right choices all week long often has the confidence to take the big swing, make the great set, or dig the tough ball when the game is on the line.

Two points better is not just philosophy, either. When I think back on some of the greatest matches I have been involved in at Nebraska, most of them come down to just a handful of points.

While I was not using "Two points better" as a mantra in my earliest years at Nebraska, some of our epic matches over the years were nevertheless good preparation for me to seeing its power. Perhaps the most dramatic example came in a match during my first year as the Huskers' head coach.

In 2000 we headed to Manhattan, Kansas, to face Kansas State and close out the regular season. We were 28-0 and the Wildcats had only ever beaten Nebraska volleyball one time. But we were missing our All-American outside hitter Laura Pilakowski, who had had an appendectomy the week of the game. We survived that match, thanks in large part to freshman Anna Schrad, who led us in kills and helped us overcome dropping the second and third sets.

That's when we hatched the dream catcher idea, because it was obvious our team was dealing with the weight of being undefeated. Still, we were the top overall seed in the national tournament and had earned the right to host the first two rounds. Laura was still trying to come back from her surgery, so our hope was that we might be able to use her sparingly, if at all, and still be okay in the first 2 sets.

We got Laura in for a handful of points, playing front row only, during a first-round sweep of Princeton. That set up a meeting with

South Carolina. The Gamecocks jumped out to an early lead in the first set, but we pulled away late for a 15–11 win. South Carolina again took an early lead in the second set, but this time the Gamecocks held on, 15–9.

We went into the break 1-1, but I thought we were still in good shape. Then South Carolina came out and opened the third set by racing to an 11–1 lead. At that point Laura came up to me and said, "Put me in." I did not want to use Laura, hoping the time off would have her at full strength for the regional round, but we were in danger of not reaching regionals so I knew we had to make something happen.

Laura entered the game and, behind her 5 kills, the team immediately went on a 7–2 run. It sparked the whole team, and, after 4 straight ace serves from Angie Oxley, we were within one at 14–13. South Carolina, however, was the one that was 2 points better that set, and they closed us out to put us on the brink of elimination.

In the fourth game we were down 12–8 when Anna stepped to the service line and ripped off 6 serves, as we finished on a 7–0 run to stay alive. Her play over that three-match stretch from Kansas State to South Carolina, with Laura seeing only limited playing time, was some of the gutsiest work I have ever seen from a freshman.

In set 5 we built a 6-point lead and I thought we were finally going to put South Carolina away, but the Gamecocks had one more rally left in them, pulling within 1 point at 14–13 before an attack error gave us the 2-point win. It was my first season, but I do not think I ever heard the Coliseum louder than after we closed out that match. Laura, in essentially two-and-a-half sets, had 15 kills. Anna posted a career-high 17 kills.

One year later, we were facing another two-points-better game in the NCAA Tournament. The 2001 team had lost only once that year, to eventual top-seed Long Beach State, in the third match of the season, and we had gotten through the first three rounds of the tournament without going to a fifth game. That set up a regional final in Lincoln against eighth-ranked Florida. We were on fire in the first game, winning 30–18, and took a 2–0 lead into the break after winning the second 30–24. (This was the first year of rally point scoring to 30.) It seemed like we were in great shape. But the Gators outlasted us in the third set, 30-28, and in the fourth, 30-25. That set up a decisive fifth game, the team's first of that season, with a trip to the Final Four on the line.

We had elected to redshirt Nancy Metcalf in 2000 despite the fact that she was the reigning Big 12 Player of the Year. She had missed the spring season while training with the U.S. National Team and was dealing with some injuries at the start of the season, so we decided to just give her a season to recover. She did not miss a beat when she returned, eventually earning Big 12 Player of the Year honors again. Without her in that Florida match we may not have made the 2001 Final Four.

The Gators had a 12-10 lead when Nancy, who had already been dominant, totally took over. She pounded back-to-back kills, which were followed by a Florida service error, then 2 more kills to put it at match point. It was only fitting that, after a side-out, Nancy got the decisive kill, her twenty-fifth of the match, to gives us a 15-13 win. She also had a career high 7 service aces and was second on the team with 14 digs. It was one of the more remarkable individual performances in all my years as a coach.

Many of my most memorable matches involve remarkable comebacks. A lot of them have come in the NCAA tournament, when you truly find out how well you have prepared all season long. The 2006 Regional Final against Minnesota was no exception.

We went into that match in Gainesville, Florida, as the top-ranked team in the country, with a 30-1 record. Minnesota was ranked ninth and on its way to becoming the Big Ten powerhouse it would be a decade later. That was also the first year Omaha was set to host the Final Four. Unlike 2015, when we embraced Destination Omaha, we had never been through the rankings pressure before in 2006. Tickets for that Final Four in downtown Omaha went on sale the same day as a Paul McCartney concert. The volleyball tickets sold out first, making Nebraska one of the few places where volleyball is bigger than a Beatle. That is the sort of weight the team was carrying. There was clearly a lot of pressure to get to the first Final Four hosted in our home state, and it showed in the first 2 matches. Our players were uptight and Minnesota blew us out in the first 2 sets, 30–25 and 30–22.

"This thing is over," I thought, as we headed to the locker room at the break. For all the success Nebraska had had to that point, there were two things the program had never done: win a regional final outside the state of Nebraska and rally from an 0-2 deficit in the NCAA Tournament. We were going to have to do both to get to Omaha.

The team came out of the locker room for the third set playing like it knew it was too close to reaching Omaha to go out without a fight. A 9–9 game turned into a 16–10 lead for Nebraska, thanks to really strong serving from Rachel Schwartz and Tracy Stalls. The Gophers went on a small run of their own after that, but we eventually pulled away to win 30–20. We started out strong in game 4, racing to an 11–3 lead, but Minnesota would not go away, pulling the set to 22–20 before we extended our lead late, for a 30–25 win. In all four games the difference in points scored was, you guessed it, two points.

Getting back to even during the match made all the difference. We opened set 5 with 5 quick points and the game never got closer than that, ending on a Sarah Pavan kill, for a 15–9 win.

All these years later, a couple of things really stick out to me about that match. First, the mental strength it took for that team to come back while everyone in the arena knew the first Final Four in Nebraska was looking like it was going to be Husker-free after 2 sets. Second, it was a total team effort. Jordan Larson and Sarah Pavan, both First Team All-Americans that season, combined for 41 kills. Dani Mancuso, who would send me the greatest text of my career a week later before facing Stanford, had a season-high 15 kills. Dani Busboom tied for the team lead with 17 digs. Rachel Holloway, a freshman, set what was then a career high with 65 assists and had some huge serves to start off set 5. Rachel Schwartz, that team's serving specialist, had 3 critical aces and her serving came into play again a week later in Omaha.

Serving is the number one way to tell how confident somebody is. It is just the player and the ball. There is no setter, no blocking; just the server and the ball. Get it over the net and there is a 900-square-feet area over there to put to your advantage. You could land a helicopter in an area that size, which I will occasionally tell my players. However, in a close match sometimes that net gets really big for servers to overcome.

That was not the case for Rachel Schwartz in the title game in 2006. Rachel walked on to the team in 2005 after a stellar career just across town at Lincoln East High School. I remember watching her play in the high school state basketball tournament at the Devaney Center and it was clear to me she was just fearless. That was in addition to being a PrepVolleyball.com All-American as a senior.

Rachel showed up and played in 30 matches for us as a true freshman defensive specialist. She played in every match as a sophomore in 2006, emerging as our serving specialist. That season she had 481 service attempts and just 19 service errors. In general I want our service-error rate to be around 7 or 8 percent. Rachel's service-error rate that season was 3.95. Needless to say, I felt pretty good when we had Rachel serving to beat Stanford and win the 2006 national title.

You already know how good the 2006 Stanford team was and what led up to the match. It was classic "two points better" every match, exactly the way a national-title match should be. We took a 23–21 lead in the first set before Stanford ripped off 5 consecutive points to pull away for a 30–27 win. The roles were reversed in set two, with our team going on a late run to overcome a 22–21 deficit and win 30–26. The third set was more championship-level volleyball, with both teams hitting better than .300. We rallied from being down 4 to go on an 8–2 run and take the third set 30–28.

That put Stanford in a pretty tough spot, needing to win the next 2 sets in front of an absolutely electric crowd of 17,000-plus. Our fans could feel that we were close to doing something that had not happened in fifteen years—win the national title as the host institution—and we rode that energy to a 24–18 lead in the fourth set. Stanford closed the gap a little bit, but a Dani Mancuso kill made it 29–25.

In to serve went Rachel, the sophomore walk-on from Lincoln who had essentially bulled her way into the regular rotation. She floated the ball toward the back line, it dipped late and landed an inch out of bounds, maybe two. If you go back and watch the telecast of that game, it is almost impossible to tell without replay if the ball was in or out and the ESPN broadcasters cannot believe Stanford had the guts to let it go. It was that close.

I could not believe Rachel served out on match point. One of our rules with serving is that you always serve in on match point. Her error made it 29–26. The Cardinal got a block after that to make it 29–27 and I called a time-out to calm everyone down and call a play. We called it for Jordan Larson, who blistered a shot down the line and off a Stanford defender for the national title.

After the celebration and the hugs and the trophy presentation, I pulled Rachel aside. "Rachel, what happened?" I asked. "All you had to do was serve it in."

"Coach," she said, "I was going for an ace."

I laughed a little, but it was a really beautiful moment. Rachel had the confidence to try to end a match for the national title on her serve. She believed she could be the last point better and she was inches away from doing it. I wish she would have remained mindful of our rules in that instance, but I will take that kind of fearless player a thousand times over. As I mentally trace it back, that may have been the start of "two points better."

Serves from a walk-on played a big part in our next national title in 2015. Much like Rachel had, another walk-on from Lincoln worked her way into the rotation as a defensive and serving specialist as a true freshman. She appeared in 29 matches in 2014 and took on an even bigger role as a sophomore the following season, emerging as a player we could count on in a national championship match.

As we prepared to face Texas in Omaha for the 2015 national title, I pulled the freshman walk-on aside before the match. I often talk about the art and science of coaching. You have to be able to balance both, and I thought this was a moment for art. Texas was one of four teams that had beaten us that season, and, hoping to give this player a little extra push, I told her she was going to have to get us 2 aces that night. I don't know why I said it, other than that I felt it. It was just a coaching instinct.

Her moment came in the second set. We had won the first 25–23, but neither team led by more than 3 points at any moment. The second set was the same, yo-yoing back and forth until we had a 14–13 lead and I sent the freshman in to serve. She hit a picture-perfect serve that died right on the back line. Texas argued it was out, the line judge signaled it was in. Her second serve was another beauty, knuckling toward the sideline and forcing a diving dig attempt that fell between two Longhorns. Time-out Texas.

The Longhorns rallied back from the 16–13 lead those two serves had given us, but the precision of those 2 points were an indication that the team was locked in. I really thought those points broke open the match. We went on to win the second game 25–23.

Two points better? The freshman walk-on from Lincoln was that night. The 2 aces were her only 2 points of the match, but they helped create a mind-set within that match that would power us to a national title.

We talk often about national championship points at Nebraska. It is another method we use to drive our training and decision making: Are we doing everything we can to be the team that is ready and able to win national championship points? Those types of points are not limited to actual title games, and every team will encounter them throughout the season. They are high-pressure points, points where you have to gut out a long rally or make an extra-effort play. These are the points that will require a team to play without fear and execute perfectly in the defining moments of a match. You are going to have to win a handful of those to even get to the actual championship point.

The four actual championship points Nebraska has had, however, comprise one of my favorite pieces of Husker trivia because, taken together, they form a pretty interesting story of Nebraska's history with the sport of volleyball. In 1995 Terry Pettit's team won Nebraska's first national title when Christy Johnson, a two-time All-American from Omaha, and Allison Weston, a Papillion native and the National Player of the Year in 1995, combined on a block. You could not write a better ending to the story of a school's first national championship in volleyball, just the second for a school east of California at that time, than to have two home-state players deliver the championship point.

It happened again in 2000. Laura Pilakowski, a Columbus, Nebraska, native, delivered the kill off a rally to beat Wisconsin. Laura was one of the greatest athletes the state of Nebraska has ever produced. Her dad coached her at Columbus and she was an okay volleyball player coming out of high school, but she was a freak athlete. There was a scouting service back then that was run by Bill Feldman. They ranked each of the players on a one-through-five scale. Only a handful of players were fives each year, but Laura earned a five-plus. Feldman told me that was the highest grade he had ever given out when she signed with Nebraska. There was a lot of hype surrounding Laura and she struggled through some position moves early in her career, so I took a lot of joy in the fact that she was the one to score the final point.

It was my first year coaching at Nebraska, but Laura was emblematic of the type of player that has been the source of so much of our success. She was a small-town girl and part of that 40 percent of players from Nebraska who make up most of our teams. She also met the 60-percent rule, as she was the daughter of a coach. She was a terror in training and displayed incredible mental toughness to battle through some early setbacks. The championship point she scored was also historically significant because it was the last point scored in NCAA volleyball with side-out scoring. (After that, the rules changed to feature games with rally scoring to 30.)

That scoring system lasted until 2006, so the championship point Jordan Larson scored that season against Stanford was the last of the 30-point era. Jordan hailed from Hooper, Nebraska, which is about as small-town as you can get, which kept the streak of Nebraskans scoring the final point alive.

I remember that point mostly because it was executed perfectly. Following Rachel Schwartz's near-miss serve, Stanford scored another point to make it 29–27. I called a time-out and called a play for Jordan. We knew where Stanford was likely to serve and we ran a go-set for Jordan. She went high line off the block, just like she had been trained to do, and put it down the line where nobody could dig it. It was a perfect play and we executed it perfectly.

Nebraska's fourth national championship point? That one was *not* scored by a Nebraskan, which is a story unto itself.

11

Never Stop Coaching

"All players will let you down at some point. You have
to decide which ones are worth it."—JOHN COOK

The conversation with my assistants after the 2013 season was the kind
of conversation every coach tries to avoid. As we were taking stock of
the previous year and looking to 2014, we started talking about per-
sonnel and one of our outside hitters, Kelsey Fien. The consensus?
She was an RM—a recruiting miss.

Kelsey was a recruiting coup for us out of high school. A six-foot-
three-inch outside hitter from Bakersfield, California, she was the
first player in her high school's history to tally 1,000 kills and probably the best player Bakersfield had ever produced. PrepVolleyball.com
ranked her as the nineteenth-best player in the class of 2012 and the
fifth-best player in California. We thought Kelsey was going to come
in and right away have a big impact as a true freshman.

Instead, she was a reserve her first two years. She played in 14
matches as a true freshman in 2012, and 11 matches during her sophomore year. We discussed redshirting Kelsey, but what was the point?
If she was not playing as a sophomore, why keep her around for an
extra year? Ultimately we decided we were just going to let her keep
playing and redouble our coaching efforts. We made the decision to
keep coaching her with the same level of expectation and put her in
increasingly tough drills in the hope of building her confidence.

We have something at Nebraska that we call the trash can drill. I
like to think of it as volleyball's equivalent to the infamous "Okla-

homa drill" in football. The Oklahoma drill has many variations, but it is essentially a one-on-one test of wills. Two players line up in a confined area and the first player to block the other to the ground or out of the area wins the drill.

The trash can drill is actually one-on-seven. We put one hitter against a defense that includes four defenders and three blockers. We will often use our male practice players as blockers, so it is really the biggest, toughest block you can find. The score starts at 10–10 and we then give the hitter a series of less-than-perfect sets. She must get to 15 and win by 2. The defense scores with a successful dig and if the defense gets to fifteen first, the score goes back to 10–10 and the drill continues.

I happened to come up with the drill as a way to coax more out of another player, Lindsey Licht. Lindsey was a six-foot-five-inch left-handed outside hitter from Colorado. She was a shy girl and played timidly early in her career. One day at practice I was so frustrated with her that we ended practice at the Coliseum and went over to the Devaney Center pool, where I had Lindsey jump off the high dive. She got up on the board, ten meters above the water, and literally crawled to the edge on her hands and knees. The rest of team was cheering and offering support and I think that's ultimately what willed her off the diving board.

That got us a little further down the road with Lindsey, but there was still work to be done. At another practice I realized I needed to send her to a place she did not think she could get out of and then let her get out of it. Thus the trash can drill was born.

Lindsey kept losing the drill. After about twenty-five minutes she finally won and went straight to the trash can next to the court and lost her lunch. She was there with her head hanging in the trash can while the rest of us were looking at each other and thinking, "Now that was a great drill."

A new drill was born that day and we had to name it, as we do every drill. Since that first time it has been known as the trash can drill. It changed Lindsey's whole mind-set about the kind of player she could be. By the time she was a senior Lindsey was a First Team All-Big 12 honoree and a Second Team All-American.

The trash can drill is a point of pride. Every day we have a full practice, we put somebody "in the trash can." It is amazing what the players do when they get in it. When we would put Kadie Rolfzen in the drill, I would swear that her vertical leap increases by a foot. She would light up at the prospect of increased competition and having to beat seven players all by herself. I do not remember how many times over her career that she got five straight kills and the drill would be over, but it was a lot.

Andie Malloy joined our program in 2016 as a graduate transfer from Baylor. She only had one season left to play, so going into the trash can became an important rite of passage for her. The first two times she did it, I could see her nerves take over. She was almost hyperventilating at the prospect of spending 15 or 20 minutes in the drill. It is a pressure-packed situation. Every time the player loses, it just gets harder and harder. It is like you are climbing up a hill then slipping down and the top is getting farther and farther away.

The first few times we put Kelsey in the trash can drill were pretty rough on her. There were some tears and she got pretty angry with me. But I refused to let her quit before getting to fifteen. I kept telling her she could do it, and eventually she accessed something beyond what she thought she was capable of and finished the drill. As is often the case, when you can show a player what she is truly capable of, it sticks with her. The gains are not always immediate. Putting someone in the trash can drill is not like flipping a switch. But you will see it eventually. When a situation looks impossible, when you need a player to access the absolute most she is capable of, that's when you most need to have shown her just what that sort of effort looks like. For Kelsey Fien, the switch flipped in the middle of her junior season.

By our standards the 2014 season got off to a rough start. We opened the year ranked No. 7 and were hosting the AVCA College Volleyball

Showcase to start the season. We lost in five sets to No. 13 Florida State in the first match of the season, and then we got swept by No. 3 Stanford two days later. It was the first time since I had taken over at Nebraska that a team started a season 0-2.

Almost a month after that opening weekend we lost to No. 2 Texas. We opened October with a win over No. 3 Penn State, but then we lost to an unranked Ohio State team the next day. We went 2-2 over our next four matches, which included losses to Michigan, also unranked, and No. 15 Illinois. We were 11-6 and ranked fourteenth as we headed to Minneapolis to face No. 25 Minnesota.

The Gophers took the first two sets as we tallied a combined 13 hitting and 6 service errors. Clearly needing a spark, I went to Kelsey off the bench early in the third set and she came up with a huge kill when we were down 12–8 and then she had another one when we trailed 16–14. At 19–19 Kelsey recorded 3 straight kills and eventually we pulled away to win 25–21. Kelsey had 7 kills in the pivotal third set and hit .700. She finished the match with 14 total kills.

After the match I was asking myself what had just happened. We started Kelsey the next match, and she kept rolling, all the way through the remainder of conference play. She ended up hitting .303 in Big Ten matches, the top mark on the team, and earned All-Conference honors.

As a coaching staff we could not believe it. The RM had become an Honorable Mention All-American. Kelsey's play over the second half of her junior season earned her a spot as a full-time starter in 2015 and her play never really trailed off after that. We faced No. 11 Oregon on its home floor in our fifth match of the season. The Ducks jumped out to a two-set lead, but a career-high 19 kills from Kelsey helped us work our way back into it and get the win and earned her a spot on the all-tournament team. A year and a day removed from her breakthrough match against Minnesota in 2014, Kelsey again had a dominant match against the Gophers in October. She matched her career-high with 19 kills against Minnesota in 2015. It was not quite enough for us to get the win, but Kelsey showed again that she was capable of carrying us when needed. That was also the weekend that we lost to Wisconsin the next night but it really spurred our championship run that season, and Kelsey played a major role.

Why did the light suddenly go on for Kelsey? That is always a tough question for any coach to answer. If it were easy, we would all simply use the technique that worked at the first sign of a player who was not reaching his or her potential. But it is rarely clear why a player's development may be lagging or what to do about it.

In some cases the hurdle is physical. You recruit players that you believe have the tools to compete at the highest level, but in all but a few cases you are banking on some physical development that you believe will come about as a result of training methods. No matter how dialed in you think those methods may be, individual athletes are always going to respond at least somewhat differently to them. The best strength and conditioning program in the world is still largely dependent upon the athletes' willingness to buy into the system and do the work that is required. Some players take to it right away and you can start seeing gains after six months of work on strength and conditioning. Others seem to hit a point, usually around their sophomore or junior year, when they realize that if they are going to get as much benefit from the program as possible, they need to start working harder. Even when you try to control as much of that as you can, there is still only so much you can do when you know the program works.

In many more cases, however, the primary hurdle seems to be mental, and that is a more difficult problem to diagnose because there are countless possible underlying reasons. For the high school All-American club team star, being surrounded by athletes that are as good or better than her can create a crisis of confidence. We now devote a lot of time and energy to figuring out ways to help our players deal with failure. Often it is something totally foreign to them coming out of high school, but we know they are going to experience it in college and we know we better have a plan to deal with it. Those efforts seem to become more vital each year as more players seem less equipped to handle setbacks. The old-school approach, "Welcome to the big leagues, kid, now figure it out," simply does not work any more.

Another thing we occasionally see when players reach the college level is a willingness to relax or be distracted. For the player who is good enough to earn a scholarship to a place like Nebraska, most of her young life has probably been focused on one thing: volleyball. She went to the camps, did all of the club tryouts, traveled to all of tournaments, and perhaps even selected a high school based on its ability to maximize her chances at earning a scholarship. A clear destination was in mind.

So what happens when that lifelong goal has been reached? What happens when you add all of the distractions of college life—living on your own, making new friends, being surrounded by multi-million-dollar facilities, adjusting to athlete status, enjoying a new social life—on top of that sense of accomplishment? For some players volleyball just starts to matter less. The coach that can recognize this needs to come up with a way to give this kind of player a new direction, and it often needs to be something more than just an attitude of "Let's go win a bunch of matches and some championships."

We tell our players stories of past players and we are pretty blunt. We want them to know right from the start that they never want to become an RM. We take preemptive measures like this, but because problems can be so varied, the only fail-safe solution I have found is to never stop coaching. Try different tactics. Create a drill like the trash can drill that directly addresses the key issue. Keep your expectations for the struggling player as high as your expectations for the player who bought in immediately, was a weight-room warrior, and is a leader on the court and off.

One of the most rewarding experiences you can have as a coach is seeing players realize for themselves what they are truly capable of achieving. It will remind you why you got into coaching in the first place. You never know when that will come. You never know when you will ask the player you considered a career backup to take the biggest swing of the season.

With a de facto home crowd behind us we had Texas down 2 sets to none in the 2015 national championship match, but the Longhorns were not going away without a fight. We came out of the break and Texas quickly jumped out to a 3-0 lead. We went on a quick run to make it 4-4, and from there on it was exactly what you'd expect of championship-level volleyball: tied at 8-8, then again at 12-12, then 13-12 Texas.

Eventually the Longhorns' errors began to mount in the must-win third set. We took advantage and found ourselves up 24-19. We were 1 point away and we were going to get five chances to win the match. Texas fought off 2 match points to make it 24-21. I called a time-out to set up a play.

In a similar situation in 2006—being up by 2 and receiving the serve with the chance to win a national title with one swing—there was little question about which direction we would take with the play. Jordan Larson was a First Team All-American that season and she would be again two years later. You want players like that on your team specifically for moments like those. The play unfolded perfectly, everyone executed at a high level, and Jordan delivered with an emphatic kill.

I decided to call the same play in the same arena at the same point in the rotation nine seasons later. This time, however, we were setting it to Kelsey Fien. Texas put in a tough serve and our freshman defensive specialist had to go to the court for the dig. Her pass was long and set up a joust at the net, which our setter won. The Longhorns kept the ball up but were scrambling and tipped the ball back over the net for a free ball. This time we got a good pass to the setter and we were in system. A strong set followed and Kelsey tooled it off the Longhorns' block. Nebraska was National Champion again.

The fourth national championship match point in Husker history was the first one not scored by a Nebraskan. But it may have been the best ending yet. When you consider how far Kelsey had come to make that swing, and consider all of the belief in her—from her coaches and her teammates—that it represented, and consider all the work she had to put in to even be there, it was a near-perfect ending.

In the middle of our jubilant locker room celebration after the win, I pulled the team together specifically to point it out. It was proof that a coach should never stop coaching.

There was another moment that reminded me of the same thing the following day. The decision to redshirt our sophomore setter in 2014 had been a difficult one. Even though we thought it was the right decision for her and the program, on an emotional level it was hard to ask a player as competitive as that to sit out a year.

Late in that 2014 season, as we prepared to head to Seattle to face Washington in the NCAA regional, I sensed that it could be the toughest time for a player who cannot play. I wrote her a note on December 8, 2014:

Continue to watch and learn. Soak it all in. A year from now you will be leading our team to Omaha! Live it each day. Have a plan. Know what you need to do. Start preparing now. You will take this team to another level!—JC

That note harkens back to one of my core beliefs about coaching: who needed me that day? I could tell she did. As a redshirt she could only help us in preparation to face Washington four days later. But she was not going to be on the floor making sets, leading the team, or doing all of the things she has since proven she is so great at doing. At that specific point, when everyone was focused on the match ahead, it seemed clear to me that she needed someone to acknowledge she was a big part of our overall plan. When she could see that everything for that 2014 team was riding on a match she would not get to play in, I thought I needed to let her know that those matches were still coming for her.

After we beat Texas to win the 2015 national title, we held a celebration at the Bob Devaney Sports Center the next day. When the celebration was over, the setter asked me to hang around for a minute and she ran to her car. She returned with the note and gave it back to me. She had kept it in her car for the previous 376 days, likely seeing it each time she parked and went into the practice facility.

We hugged and it was a truly special moment. I do not know if I have ever had a player place more trust in one of my decisions than she did when she agreed to redshirt that previous season. One year later we had proof that we had done it together. It was there in the trophy that sat in our locker room and it was there in the pieces of the championship net hanging around the players' necks. Most of all it was there in the note that had found its way back to me.

12

Regrets

"Excellence is the gradual result of always striving to do better."—PAT RILEY, Hall of Fame basketball coach

It took many years of coaching for me to get to a point where my primary regrets did not stem from big losses or having a title slip through our hands or just not being good enough as a team to get it done. It was a miserable way to coach. The losses eat at you and the big wins, when they do come, are less joyful than they should be. I shook free of that way of thinking through my own personal maturity plus a renewed focus on the journey that each season presents and the opportunities that each new team brings to do it better than we have ever done it before. These two things have helped me evolve to a point where my coaching ability is not defined by wins and losses. I would love to say that it also has removed all of my regrets, but, unfortunately, if you coach long enough there will be a few decisions you made or did not make that will always stick with you.

In 1983 I was in my second year coaching volleyball at Francis Parker School. We became the first school from San Diego to make the California state playoffs and we had a chance to win the whole thing that year. We faced Newport Christian High in the state final.

One of the best players in our program that year was freshman middle blocker Tracy Hughes. I believed she was one of the school's best players, but I was hesitant to just throw her into the mix with the varsity. So Tracy led the junior varsity team and was worked into the varsity rotation whenever possible. She scored some big points for us on our way to the state tournament.

I was still a young coach at that point, however, and I had this thing in my mind that you had to play your seniors, particularly with a state title on the line. The parents expected you to play the seniors and the entire school expected you to play the seniors. It was a fairly early point in the evolution of women's sports, and by then sanctioned competitions at most schools had existed for only about a decade. It seems foolish now, but back then there was still this hesitation to make girls' sports as cutthroat and competitive as boys' sports were, as though the girls couldn't handle the pressure.

All of those things were bouncing around in my mind as we went into that match, and I did what I was expected to do: play the seniors. Newport Christian drilled us in the first set 15–3. We rallied to win the second 15–9, dropped a heartbreaker in the third, 15–13, and then got rolled 15–2 in the fourth. Tracy didn't get in the match.

She approached me after the game. "Why didn't you play me?" she asked. I did not have an answer. What could I say? Explain my mind-set behind playing the seniors? There was no explanation beyond the fact that it was the safe and expected thing to do. Not having an answer to her very direct and rational question was a defining coaching moment for me. That conservative mind-set vanished after that match.

Ever since that match in 1983 my approach has been that the best players play. I do not care if they are freshmen or seniors. I do not care who agrees or disagrees with the decision. We tell our recruits that they will have a chance to start as freshmen because it is true. If they are good enough they will play, and there are countless examples of that philosophy over the years. Most recently, Justine Wong-Orantes, Kadie Rolfzen, and Amber Rolfzen all came in as freshmen in 2013 and all three started and played in almost every match. We played a total of 408 sets during their four years at Nebraska, and those three were in the lineup for 397 of them. Each of them played right away and together they played almost every day thereafter, barring the occasional injury.

I do not know if that would be happening had I not had the experience with Tracy and the state championship in 1983. Her story has a happy ending, though. She was the epitome of the student-athlete: she carried a 4.0 grade point average while serving as the student body vice president and the editor of the yearbook. As a senior in 1986 Tracy recorded 24 kills in the state championship against San Jose's Valley Christian. We swept that match 15-7, 15-4, 15-3, and Francis Parker became the first San Diego school to win a state title. Tracy went on to play four years at Stanford. She also changed my coaching career at a very early stage.

Late in my tenure at Wisconsin I found a recruit I really thought could be something special. Sherisa Livingston was from Simi Valley, California, just north of Los Angeles. As a California native myself, I thought I could have some success luring players from there to Wisconsin. Sherisa was sort of a "project" as a high school player. USC, UCLA, and Stanford all stayed away from her, but I thought I could develop her and decided to take a shot at it.

Sherisa was raised by her mother and grew up in a single-parent household, and I could tell during my home visit that it was a tough upbringing. I sensed that a big element of getting Sherisa to reach her potential would be to earn her trust. She ended up picking Wisconsin and developed into a great player there, becoming the first player in program history to earn First Team All-America honors, something she did as both a junior and a senior.

I only got to coach her for one year, however. Sherisa was a freshman in 1998. She was a key part of that team that almost knocked off Nebraska at the Coliseum in one of the greatest regional finals ever. It was following that match when Terry Pettit told me he was getting out of coaching and asked me to come back to Lincoln.

I did, of course, and perhaps the toughest moment of making that decision was telling Sherisa. I met with her one-on-one to break the news and I am still haunted by the look of abandonment in her eyes. She had placed a great deal of trust in me when she decided to uproot her life and move halfway across the country. We had close to a father-daughter relationship and I decided I had to try and do something. I called Pettit to ask if I could bring Sherisa with me as a transfer. I explained that I had recruited her and taken care of her, and felt responsible like a father.

Pettit said we could not do it. Bringing me back to Nebraska and paying me a head coach's salary to be an associate head coach was already raising suspicions about Nebraska's future in volleyball circles. The last thing Pettit wanted was the additional controversy that would come if an outgoing coach took his best player with him to a perennial powerhouse.

In hindsight I wish I had told Pettit that Sherisa was coming with me and that it was part of the deal. Not because she was a great player, though she was, but because I knew I had let her down.

Sherisa made the most of her career at Wisconsin. I had to coach against her for a national championship in 2000. She was a junior and an All-American at that point and it is still one of the toughest matches I have ever had to coach. Nebraska won in five, but I did not enjoy having to coach against a bunch of players I had recruited to Wisconsin.

I sought out Sherisa after the match and tried to shake her hand, but she would not talk to me or even look at me. I understood that and I could not blame her. But it hurt.

After finishing her career at Wisconsin, Sherisa went on to play overseas for more than a decade in Turkey, Italy, Greece, Puerto Rico, the Netherlands, Indonesia, and Spain. In 2007 she was inducted into the Wisconsin Athletic Hall of Fame.

Near the end of Sherisa's professional volleyball career we connected on Facebook. I would send her the occasional message when I saw that her team was winning or I knew that she was playing with some other players I had coached. Eventually those conversations turned to what she was going to do once she was done playing. "Have you thought about coaching?" I asked.

"A little bit," Sherisa said. "How would I get into that?"

I asked her to join our program as a volunteer assistant and told her I would help her find a job after that. She moved to Lincoln in 2013 and we were able to repair a relationship that had basically ended thirteen years earlier. In 2014 Sherisa took a job as an assistant coach at Seattle University. In 2015 she took over a brand new program at the University of Antelope Valley in Lancaster, California, not far from her childhood home. Some regrets can be reversed.

My first year at Nebraska produced another regret that sticks with me to this day. As I wrote earlier, Laura Pilakowski was one of the greatest athletes I had ever seen coming out of high school, but as a freshman she did not have a clue about blocking at the college level. The 1999 team had two middle blockers, Amber Holmquist and Jenny Kropp, both of whom were more than capable of holding down the middle. I went to Pettit and asked him to consider redshirting Laura. "Well, there might be a time where we just need a side-out," I recall him saying. "We can put her in, set her on a slide, and she will get us a kill."

I thought it was a risky decision to burn a redshirt for that slim possibility. Laura ended up playing in nine sets that season and we did not use her enough to even include her on our NCAA tournament roster.

I had to break the news to Laura that she was not going to travel with us during the tournament. Talk about disappointing a player. The hurt shown on her face was almost too much for me to handle. She was one of the most highly regarded recruits in history, we had made the decision to play her, and now she was not even going to suit up for the tournament. Laura hated me after that.

When I took over the program in 2000 I moved her to outside hitter, she became a First Team All-American as a sophomore, the team went undefeated and won the national title, and Laura scored the final point. Still, our relationship remained iffy throughout the rest of her career.

Laura tried playing professionally for a while but she never really loved the experience. She ended up back in Lincoln and we had lunch one day, which led to her becoming our strength and conditioning coach. Much like the Sherisa Livingston story, this regret had a rewarding end.

Still, it would have been nice to have had a player like Laura for another year. Occasionally when I'm with John Baylor, the play-by-play voice of Nebraska volleyball for the past twenty-five years, together we shout to the heavens: "Why didn't we redshirt Laura!?"

If the 2007 team was the most talented team I ever coached at Nebraska, the 2005 team comes in a close second. That team featured a lot of names we have already mentioned—Dani Busboom, Jordan Larson, Sarah Pavan, Tracy Stalls, Christina Houghtelling—but it also had Melissa Elmer in the middle, one of the greatest blockers in NCAA history. Maggie Griffin, who now runs a club team in Nebraska, started at setter. Jennifer Saleaumua, one of the best all-around players I have ever coached, did a little bit of everything for us. It was a ridiculous collection of talent and it allowed us to get really creative.

We ran a 6–2 lineup that season, and they played without a libero. I called it the "ultimate system" because we had the option for all kinds of formations. We were hell to play, and we finished the regular season 33-1, with the lone loss coming in the regular season finale on the road at Texas.

We had been the top-ranked team all season and cruised through the first four rounds of the NCAA Tournament, sweeping every match. We met Santa Clara in the semifinal in San Antonio and crushed the Broncos, too. That match was over in sixty minutes. It set up a match with Washington for the national title.

On the Friday between the semifinal and final matches, the AVCA held its annual awards banquet. These things are sort of a blur for coaches who are trying to prepare for matches, so I had no idea the problems that banquet was going to cause us the next night.

When I left the banquet that Friday and walked outside, I saw Jordan Larson crying and being consoled by her mother and stepfather. She was disappointed because she lost the National Freshman of the Year award to Nicole Fawcett of Penn State.

I looked the other direction and saw Sarah Pavan crying too; she was being consoled by her father. She had lost the National Player of the Year award to her teammate, Christina Houghtelling. Not many people expected Christina to win that award, but I had a good idea she might. We played six top-ten teams that season and in those matches Christina's stats were ridiculous. Coaches notice these sorts of matches when it comes time to vote on awards. I looked around and realized Jordan was in the tank, Sarah was in the tank, and Christina was wondering what the hell had just happened.

I honestly thought they would just get over it. I underestimated how much it was going to affect our play the next night. But I was wrong and I realized it as soon as the championship match started.

Washington opened the first set by serving right at Sarah for an ace. The Huskies took a 2–0 lead on an attack error by Christina and I could tell we were out of it. I called a time-out. "This is the earliest time-out in the history of the Final Four," I told the team when they came into the huddle, hoping to draw a laugh and lighten the mood. It was not enough to shake us out of our funk.

Washington swept us to win its first national title. Jordan played the worst match of her life with only 1 kill on 20 attempts. Sarah was trying to do everything and hit pretty well at .429, but she was yelling at her teammates, trying to spur them along. Christina was dealing with the expectation of being the best player on the court, but that night she surely wasn't, hitting .079 on 38 attempts.

That was my first experience of having that much talent on one team, and I now wish that I had been more proactive as we headed into the awards banquet. I wish I would have told Jordan that it was not a given that she would win Freshman of the Year. I wish I had told Sarah and Christina that both of them deserved it but only one of them was going to win Player of the Year. More than anything, I wish I had driven home the point that we were in San Antonio to win a team championship, not individual awards.

After not doing any of those things, I was given another chance to debrief the team and deliver that message after the banquet, but I missed that opportunity too. I honestly did not sense it could be an issue. You can be sure I learned to keep an eye out for those things after that, however. Having one of the most talented teams in history fall just short of a title is not a whole lot of fun.

Recruiting your daughter, or in this case not recruiting your daughter, is a strange experience. It is hard for everyone involved to keep from blurring the lines. I had to be a father but also remain a coach. Lauren had to be a daughter but also pursue the best opportunity for herself as a player. For that reason I took a laid-back approach to trying to guide her recruiting. I would offer whatever insight I could when asked, but for the most part I played the role any father would and just wanted Lauren to have the freedom to make her own choice.

There were a lot of reasons that choice was not Nebraska when Lauren came out of high school. As a coach I honestly thought that Lauren might be too small to play setter in the Big 12. That was when she was a high school sophomore. Additionally, we were not really looking for setters in that recruiting class. Our 2009 team ended up having three on the roster, so at that point I was not really pushing Nebraska for Lauren.

I was, however, making the case that she should go to Creighton. I thought it would be perfect. She would be close to home, I would get the chance to see her play, and I knew she was good enough to sort of change that program. Lauren would have been a huge recruiting win for the Bluejays.

As a sophomore she was not interested in the volleyball recruiting process at all, which in this era of recruiting is really a key time for recruits. She was not reaching out to coaches and she sort of refused to engage in the process that early. Cincinnati, Creighton, and Kansas State were recruiting her the hardest at that point. Most players, once they get some interest from schools, jump in to recruiting head first. But Lauren was content to let things play out slowly, which is partly why she was not being heavily recruited.

Another reason, I think, was that she was my daughter. There was no question that Lauren could play. She would win national high school player and setter of the year awards while at Lincoln Pius X, but it seemed like there were some coaches out there who assumed Lauren would end up at Nebraska and simply stayed away.

That started to change in the spring of her junior year in high school after Lauren had a big club season. She got calls from UCLA and Stanford and her recruiting process started to pick up. Hawaii showed some interest, too, as did Colorado State.

Ironically, it was right around that time that I made perhaps my strongest pitch for her to attend Nebraska. Our setter situation had become a little more clearly defined, so I laid it out for her one night at dinner. "Lauren, the way this is working out, you could come to Nebraska," I said. "Why don't you really think about it?"

"No way," she said. "I grew up here, you're my dad, and there is no way I'm staying here."

That conversation lasted about half of dinner. Lauren ended up visiting Kansas State and then headed out west to visit Stanford and UCLA. The week Lauren was supposed to visit Stanford, the Cardinal offered a spot to Karissa Cook, my brother Dave's daughter and Lauren's cousin. Karissa committed to Stanford as a setter and that same week Lauren picked UCLA.

The 2009 season ended up being a strange one for UCLA. In early September the Bruins visited Lincoln for the Ameritas Players Challenge, a showcase match that we moved from the Coliseum to the Bob Devaney Sports Center. UCLA beat us in 5 sets, our first loss at home since 2004, and Lauren played great. She kept playing great throughout the entire season, earning National Freshman of the Year honors, and the Bruins ended up one swing away from winning the Pac-10.

Behind the scenes, however, the wheels were coming off the bus with that team. When Lauren came home for Christmas break after the 2009 season, she had all of her stuff with her and said she was not going back. I told her she was going back. She had made a commitment for at least a year when she signed her scholarship papers and she was going to honor that commitment.

Lauren got back to Los Angeles on January 2, 2010, and by then things had only gotten worse at UCLA. A handful of players quit the team that day. Head coach Andy Banachowski, who had coached the Bruins for forty-three years, announced his retirement on January 11, the same day he granted Lauren the scholarship release that allowed her to come back to Nebraska.

We did not have a scholarship available for Lauren, so she had to walk on. I asked her if she was going to get a job to pay for school. Her response: "I'll earn a scholarship. You'll see."

Sydney Anderson was a senior in 2010, so the addition of Lauren gave us two setters on the roster, both of whom could play at a very high level. The simplest solution to that potential problem was to redshirt Lauren. I prepared my pitch to her. At that point the Rolfzen twins had already committed to come to Nebraska and I made the case that if Lauren redshirted she could be a senior when the twins were freshmen. I thought it was a pretty good plan. However, in a conversation that went like many father-daughter talks go, Lauren shot down that idea in a hurry. "I'm not redshirting," she said. "You can play me or not play me, but I'm not redshirting."

Would you care to guess how many times since then Lauren has told me she wished she had redshirted? Let's just say it has been many. But decisions like that are hard for young athletes to understand.

We went with a 6-2 that season to utilize both our setters as well as two six-foot-five left-handed hitters, Lindsey Licht and Morgan Broekhuis. It worked well for the most part, but our chemistry was not great. We had two great setters, but Lauren and Sydney were each only playing half the time. It is not that different from what football coaches always say about playing two quarterbacks: if you have two, you don't have one.

That team still made it to the regionals, where we lost a controversial match to Washington in Seattle. In retrospect, though, I think our team would have been better running a 5-1. Sydney had earned the right to run that in her senior season. I guess that makes this a three-way regret. One, I probably should have recruited Lauren harder. If we had lined her up to come to Nebraska as a freshman, it would have been easier to get our setter recruiting in line for the years after. Two, I should have pushed harder for Lauren to redshirt. That would have given Sydney the opportunity she had earned to run the show her senior year. Three, redshirting would have allowed Lauren a chance to play with a great freshman class in 2013 that featured the Rolfzen twins and Justine Wong-Orantes.

Instead we had to go out and find a setter for 2013. We ended up getting Mary Pollmiller as a transfer from Tennessee. Ironically, Mary was on her recruiting visit to Nebraska in 2009 on the day Lauren and UCLA beat us at the Devaney Center. She came in and played well for us, earning Honorable Mention All-America honors in each of her two seasons as a Husker. Still, 2013 was her first year in the program. For a team that played three freshmen, having a senior setter would have been valuable experience.

Many of the regrets that have stuck with me over years come down to the redshirt decision. We coaches had the redshirt discussion halfway through Kelsey Fien's career and ultimately decided it was not worth it. Then Kelsey had a remarkable transformation as a player.

We operate on a 33-percent rule: a third of your players are going to be your leaders and the hardest workers. That is the top third. The middle third are just sort of there. Those players are not causing problems, but they also are content to simply follow. The bottom third, or "B3s," as we call them, consists of the players who actively cause problems. They break team rules, get in trouble, complain, and sort of take the life out of the team. We used to have a two-by-four wrapped in carpet with "B3" painted on it. A player who fell to that level had to push that board up and down the court in a bear crawl. We had some players who went to the B3 corner once, but not many of them made a second trip. You never wanted to be a B3 in our program.

Kelsey was never a B3. She was squarely in the middle third early in her career, which affected our decision not to redshirt her going into her junior year. By the end of that season, however, she had turned the corner and it was apparent that we probably should have redshirted her. I would have loved to have Kelsey on our 2016 team as a senior, but you make the best decisions you can with the information you have.

Still, there is value in sharing these stories. After our 2016 season was over, a sophomore outside hitter from Waverly, Nebraska, who played only sparingly in her first two years, told me she was going to be the next Kelsey Fien. Sometimes even your regrets can have a positive impact on the program.

Every college coach has his or her share of stories about the recruits he or she missed out on, and I am no different. There are plenty of examples over the years, but one recent one that sticks with me is Taylor Sandbothe.

Taylor was a middle blocker in the 2013 class from Lee's Summit, Missouri, just outside of Kansas City. KC is right within our recruiting wheelhouse, so I got the chance to see her play in a few tournaments in Omaha and I saw her play in Kansas City. She was on the radar of a lot of programs in the area. I think I went and watched her five different times, trying to talk myself into recruiting her, but I just could not quite get to a point where I was ready to offer Taylor a scholarship.

She was a little undersized for a middle blocker at six-foot-two, and, while athletic enough, she was not the sort of freak athlete that was impossible to ignore. Most of all, however, I just did not see the competitive fire in her that would trump some of her other weaknesses as a high school sophomore. That is one of the biggest challenges of early recruiting in volleyball: it is really hard to predict what a given player will eventually become. Based on what our staff was seeing from Taylor in matches, we decided to pass on her.

A lot of other schools in the area passed on her too. I do not know if Kansas, Missouri, Creighton, or Kansas State pursued her that hard either. Taylor signed with Ohio State, which meant I had to face her for the next four years.

She blossomed into a great player for the Buckeyes. Taylor started every match for Ohio State as a true freshman, earning Big 10 All-Freshman honors. There were still some leadership questions with her at that early stage in her career, and she actually considered transferring from Ohio State following the 2013 season. Taylor even gave Nebraska a long look. But ultimately she did not want to sit out a year as a transfer as required by Big 10 rules, so she stuck with the Buckeyes. She only got better.

We played Ohio State four times during Taylor's time in Columbus. We beat the Buckeyes her freshman season, but Ohio State beat us in 2014, 2015, and 2016. The loss to Ohio State in 2016 was our only loss at home that year and Taylor played great, recording 12 kills on .346 hitting. She grew into one of the most fun players to play against and watch. You have to tip your hat to their coaching staff for seeing something in her that others were missing.

Taylor signed a professional contract to play volleyball in France shortly after her senior season was over. It is a really great story about a kid who turned it around. Too bad that turnaround didn't happen at Nebraska.

If there is one regret that encompasses most of my coaching career, it is this: I wish I would have learned earlier to coach with love rather than anger. That is a lesson that took me a long time to learn. I started out as a football coach and that was my earliest model of how to coach. We have all seen how football coaches handle things. Many of them coach with a lot of anger. Football is a violent, harsh game. It is a sport of collisions and combat. The goal of playing football is to crush the player in front of you and crush the other team.

That approach does not work so well in volleyball. I am not even sure it works that well in football, or in any sport, for that matter. The current generation of athletes requires a different coaching approach, and it took me a while to realize that. When I first started coaching volleyball at Francis Parker, I coached those teams of girls like I would coach a football team of boys. I put them through hard drills and expected them to toughen up. It worked somewhat, but we also had players crying every once and a while. When that happened I would get called into the office and the principal would tell me, "You can't make these girls cry." I would explain that I was not even doing anything. From my perspective I thought I had scaled back from my football days and was only making an effort to toughen them up. From their perspective it was the toughest thing anyone had ever asked them to do as an athlete.

The tough approach worked for me for a while. My first team at Nebraska in 2000 had players like Lindsay Peterson and Jenny Kropp, two tough small town girls who could handle anything. In fact, they seemed to thrive when I amped up the pressure on them.

At some point, however, I made the decision to coach with love rather than anger. I think it is a constant battle for most coaches and it is something I still struggle with to this day. I am constantly drifting back and forth over the line that separates the two. You have to train yourself to manage your reactions, because coaches are always going to get angry. You get angry with your players. Why can't you do this? You get angry with your assistants. Why aren't we playing well?

I coached for a long time like that before realizing that it did not have to be that way. I had a choice to make when I walked into the gym every day: I could coach with love or I could coach with anger. I could be in the moment every day and remember why I wanted to do this in the first place. I could marvel at all of the amazing athletes I was getting to work with and really be grateful for the opportunity we get each season to take a group of players, coaches, and staff and try to make our dreams come true.

The other option? I could focus on every practice failure. I could take every loss personally. I could try to eliminate mistakes through fear. Every coach gets to make that choice. I write daily reminders to myself to make sure I am choosing to be the coach I want to be. I wish I had recognized sooner that the choice was up to me.

13

Is God a Coach?

*"They will soar on wings like eagles; they will run and not
grow weary; they will walk and not be faint."*—ISAIAH 40:31

If I have learned anything from a lifetime of watching and coaching
sports, it is that they are almost impossible to separate from spirituality. We see constant examples of it every single day—the athlete who
thanks God in a postgame interview, the player taking a quiet moment
to kneel and pray before a big game, two teams coming together after
a game to pray together. Spirituality is so deeply embedded in sports
that we almost expect to see those things when watching the games
we love. How else are we supposed to understand the devastating
heartbreak or pure joy that sports can produce?

My ongoing study of great coaches has only turned up more examples. I remember watching an interview with Duke basketball coach
Mike Krzyzewski once, when he revealed that he coaches with a rosary
in his pocket. Legendary UCLA basketball coach John Wooden created one of the founding documents of coaching when he created his
"Pyramid of Success." At the very top of Wooden's hierarchy—above
poise and confidence, condition and skill, friendship and loyalty—are
two triangles that make up the point of the pyramid. The triangle on
the left includes the words "Faith (through prayer)"; the triangle on
the right reads "Patience (good things take time)." Wooden was perhaps the greatest team sports coach in history and faith clearly played
a big role in how he chose to lead.

Examples like that have always left me to wonder if God is a coach. From my perspective, God certainly has a lot of coach-like traits. God asks us to be disciplined, treat others the way we want to be treated, and believe in something greater than ourselves. Those are all things we do as coaches as we try to build a culture.

God asks us to rebuild and improve our faith each year. This is the same thing we ask of our athletes and of ourselves as coaches. A golfer breaks down his swing over the winter. A basketball player shoots thousands of jump shots and works on her footwork in the offseason. A coach reinvents himself.

God coaches by rebuilding us and giving us more reps. God is constantly teaching us new lessons and new ways to remain humble. God helps us believe in ourselves, erases our doubts, and provides a sense of hope when we fail or do not perform our best. Couldn't you say all of the same things about sports? They are all things I have experienced in a lifetime devoted to athletics and competition.

There have been many people over the years who have helped me incorporate spirituality into my leadership philosophy. Tom Osborne and one of his close spiritual advisors, Fred Kauffman, were great examples for me, as was one of Osborne's assistants, Ron Brown. Jeff Duke, a former assistant football coach at Florida State, wrote a book, *3D Coach*, which had a great impact on me. In the book Duke outlines the three dimensions of coaching. The first dimension is being fundamentally sound in the skills and strategies of the sport you coach. Many people stop there. The second involves coaching the mind and the methods you use to motivate your players and teams. The third is spiritual and involves capturing an athlete's heart. That was a message that rang true to me and I incorporated it into my philosophy.

Chris Bubak, a former Nebraska football player who became the state director of the Nebraska chapter of the Fellowship of Christian Athletes, was instrumental in helping blend elements of spirituality into how I coached. He helped me create my own pyramid, adapted specifically to fit Nebraska volleyball, as a guide. Chris was also masterful at giving examples from the bible or from a sermon and then backing those up with real-world examples that apply to teams. It was a way to appeal to players of all faiths, which is an important consideration for any coach. You will often find when you look at coaches' inner circles that they include someone who can bring a spiritual dimension to the team within the team. It has certainly been true for my career and it is another viewpoint that can help you gain a better understanding of motivation and teambuilding.

We see things in sports that cannot be explained, from great plays to crushing defeats. We watch heavy favorites do everything in their power to win and yet they still fall short. Sometimes it is beyond imagination. Do these moments come from God? I know a lot of people believe that.

Is God coaching us? There have been many moments over the course of my career when I have been powerless to come up with any other explanation.

Alicia Ostrander was a good high school volleyball player from Gordon in Nebraska's panhandle, but she was an even better basketball player. In fact, most of her best offers to play in college were for basketball. But she had a dream to play volleyball at Nebraska. Alicia never played club volleyball, so all I knew about her was videotape of high school matches. I watched the tape and told her she would be passing up some great opportunities if she chose to play volleyball over basketball. She was determined, however. There was something in her that would not be denied, so we offered her a walk-on spot and she joined our program in 2011.

Having not played much volleyball to that point compared to her peers, Alicia was pretty far behind when she arrived at Nebraska. It was hard for us to even get her into drills because she had so far to go. But she stuck out a redshirt year her freshman season, and we found an opportunity that summer for her to go to Tianjin, China, with Li Shan, a Chinese coach who spent a couple of months observing our program during the 2012 season. I thought it would be a way for Alicia to sort of catch up to the other players on the team and so she wouldn't have to go halfway across the world by herself, I called up Kirsten Bernthal Booth, the head coach at Creighton, and asked her if she had any players who might be interested in going. Leah McNary, an outside hitter who became an all-conference player for the Bluejays, made the trip, too.

Training in China is highly regimented. Alicia and Leah arrived, moved into a dorm, and for the next two weeks approached volleyball like it was their job. Monday through Friday they practiced for three hours in the morning and four in the afternoon. Over twelve total days they put in about seventy hours of volleyball. It was instrumental in Alicia's development. The next season Alicia played in a handful of matches and came up with a pivotal block in the fifth set of a win over Michigan State.

Alicia was always a great athlete. Over the course of her career she played the middle, then the right side, then back to the middle, then to the left side. She was athletic enough to play every position on the front row. Maybe it should not have been a total surprise, then, that she found some of her greatest success in the sand.

The next step in Alicia's development came when we started a beach volleyball program, the first in the Midwest, in the spring of 2013. She was a great sand player right away, working her way onto one of our top two teams. Alicia became so good in sand that after the 2015 beach season she started getting offers to be a graduate transfer and play at some of the biggest beach programs in the country, including Arizona, Arizona State, and a couple of Florida schools.

She turned them all down. I told her she was crazy, but Alicia was determined to finish out her senior season of indoor volleyball. She also had another dream she wanted to chase: Alicia planned to play basketball at Nebraska for one season after the 2015 volleyball season was over.

There are not a lot of athletes out there who could even consider such a dream, but it did not surprise me that Alicia was one to try it. Her teammates named her a captain in 2015 and she contributed to our national-title team that season. Ten days after volleyball season was over, Alicia reported to basketball practice, where she ruptured her Achilles tendon on the first day.

When I ask if God is a coach, Alicia often comes to mind. Why did she come to Nebraska? What if she had not? Where did she find the fearlessness to believe she could do anything? Alicia was not a player who was really open with her spirituality. Just like everyone, some athletes are and some are not. But what I saw in her was what I often see in some of our openly spiritual players: a strength that seemed to come from some source greater than herself. Alicia felt she had the power to achieve anything. Where did she get that power? Examples like that, questions I cannot necessarily answer, always bring me back to the question I have asked throughout my entire career: Is God a coach?

Jordan Wilberger was another walk-on from Nebraska's panhandle whose success was tough to explain through any conventional ideas. Jordan was from Scottsbluff and sort of fit that classic western Nebraska profile: a multisport athlete who hadn't played a ton of club volleyball. She had offers to play at some smaller schools, but Jordan opted to take Nebraska's walk-on offer.

We redshirted Jordan in 2007 and were bringing her along slowly as a freshman in 2008 when she suddenly got thrust into the spotlight. She only played in 6 of our first 27 matches as a backup middle blocker . Brooke Delano, also a redshirt freshman in 2008, was our top backup in the middle in addition to serving a utility role for the team. Brooke went down with a season-ending injury on November 12 against Missouri. Kori Cooper, our starter, who was having the best season of her career at that point, suffered a season-ending knee injury a week later. All of a sudden we were down to two middle blockers on the roster—Jordan and Amanda Gates.

There was nothing about Jordan's experience that said she would step into the lineup two weeks before the tournament and we would not miss a beat, but that is exactly what happened. She had her best offensive match of the season in the first round of the NCAA Tournament against Liberty. She led us in blocks the next night in a second-round win over Alabama-Birmingham. From there we headed off to Seattle for the regional.

I do not know that Jordan ever imagined she would play so many huge points in her first year, much less over the course of her career, but she stared the final 7 matches of that season and proved she could do it again in 2008. It is a long shot for any walk-on, but over the next three seasons she continued to earn more and more playing time. She was named a captain as a senior in 2011 and served as one of our spiritual leaders throughout her career. When we had to use her in 2008, she stepped up and did her job well, playing at a level I did not know she was capable of. Jordan got the strength to do that from somewhere.

She manned the middle for us in that 2008 regional as we swept Michigan in the semifinal. That set up a huge match against Washington on its home court, which may be the best proof I have seen yet of a true miracle moment, this one involving the other Jordan on that team.

Jordan Larson's mother, Kae Clough, made the trip to Washington to watch us in the regional, despite the fact that she was undergoing chemotherapy for breast cancer. Kae watched our first match against Michigan, but the trip had taken a toll; she stayed in the hotel room to watch on television the next night against Washington.

We dropped the first 2 sets to the Huskies, fought back to win the next 2, including a gutty 26–24 win in the fourth, setting up a winner-take-all fifth set. Washington punched us in the mouth early with a raucous crowd behind them, building a 3–0 lead. I called a time-out. The lead grew to 6–1 before we scored back-to-back points to make it 6–3, but then the Huskies reeled off 3 straight points to make it 9–3. Washington was already punching their ticket to Omaha. I called a time-out, and what happened next was one of the most amazing things I have ever seen in the sport of volleyball.

We called a play for Jordan out of the time-out. She appeared to have something extra on her jump and smashed the ball down for her first kill of the set to make it 9–4. At 9–6 Jordan rolled one over the block to make it 9–7. Next play she smashed one off the block to cut the lead to 1, at 9–8. Washington then gave us a free ball, which Jordan promptly put away at the net. Tie game. Two points later, Jordan came up with a block to make it 12–9 and an almost unheard of 9-point run.

Washington battled back to make it 13–13, but hit out to set up match point. Jordan went back to serve and drilled an ace. Nobody touched it.

I still do not believe what I saw that night. We recorded 6 kills in that set and Jordan had the last 5, to go along with a block and the ace that ended the match. There is no other way to put it: she willed us to win. Jordan was not going to let our season end in Seattle. Not with her mother so close by, though unable to attend. I truly believe it was a miracle. Jordan wanted her mother to have one more chance to watch her play, and she got to in Omaha a week later where we gave Penn State, the eventual National Champion, the toughest match it had faced all season. Kae Clough passed away nine months after that match.

Is God a coach? Sometimes "Yes" is the only explanation that makes sense.

14

Ultimate Trust

"We do not rise to the level of our expectations, we fall
to the level of our training."—ARCHILOCUS, Greek poet

When I was worried that I had lost a little joy for coaching between
the 2008 and 2009 seasons, I decided I was going to do one of two
things to shake me out of my funk. I have been a lifelong music lover,
so I thought about learning to play guitar. The other option was to get
my pilot's license.

My fascination with aviation goes way back, too. Growing up in
San Diego, the military presence was everywhere. I was still living
there and coaching at Francis Parker when the film *Top Gun* came
out. That movie made me want to become a pilot. Some of the guys I
played beach volleyball with were in the training program, so I went
to the Navy recruiting office one day and asked the recruiter, "Can I
be a Top Gun pilot?" I was ready to do it.

One small snag: I was too tall. They need short guys to fit in the
cockpit. But they said I could fly cargo planes with no problem. I was
not doing that. Once I knew the jets were out, I left and it was back
to coaching.

Coaching eventually led me back to planes, though. It never hurts
for a college coach to have access to a plane, and I did through my
friend Todd Duncan, chairman of Duncan Aviation in Lincoln. Todd
is also a volleyball supporter. He has occasionally flown me to speaking engagements and impromptu recruiting visits.

One of my first flights with Todd was in 2002. I got a call that fall from Judy Mousel, the volleyball coach at Cambridge High School in southwest Nebraska. She told me she had a player, Christina Hough-telling, who I needed to come take a look at. I was skeptical. Christina was a tall, gangly kid who was a great athlete and had come to one of our camps earlier in her high school career. But she was pretty rough around the edges when it came to volleyball. She was not even on our radar. Mousel was insistent.

"I've been coaching here for twenty-five years," she told me over the phone. "I would never call you if I didn't think I had a kid who could play for the Huskers." I took her word for it and called Todd to see if he could fly me out to Cambridge. He was up for it, so I met him at the airport and away we went.

A lot of people do not know that almost all of these towns, no matter how small, have an airport somewhere close by that services the town. These rural airports always have courtesy cars and for some reason it is usually a beat-up old Lincoln Town Car. When you get there you always know there will be a car waiting for you to use to get where you need to go. When you're done with it you pay for the gas and fly out.

Todd and I got to Cambridge a few hours before the match, so we headed into town. We found a cafe and decided to grab a bite to eat. The place where we ended up offered a hamburger, fries, and Coke for $2.99. It was as quintessentially a small-town Nebraska experience as you could find. I felt like I had stepped back into the 1950s.

While we were eating our burgers, a man by the name of Stew Minnick walked in with a Labrador retriever. He was a local legend and a lifelong supporter of athletics in Cambridge, particularly baseball. Stew had contracted polio in the 1930s during the national epidemic and walked with a limp, but that had not kept him from running track in high school. He attended the University of Nebraska, graduated with an accounting degree, and returned to Cambridge to be a bookkeeper and coach Legion baseball. He started going to Husker football games in the 1950s as a season ticket holder and eventually ended up with enough tickets that he would take his entire baseball team to Husker home games when he could. Stew was plenty familiar with Nebraska athletics, so it was not a surprise when he recognized us.

After he went to the counter to buy an ice cream cone, he stopped by our table, assuming we were in town for the big match. We got to talking and Stew is standing there with his dog at his feet and the ice cream is starting to melt. We talked for ten or fifteen minutes and the whole time I just watched as ice cream slowly dripped down his hand. We wrap up our conversation and Stew flipped his ice cream cone into the air and the Labrador jumped up and wolfed it down in one bite. Welcome to Cambridge.

We went to the match, it was a packed house, and Christina played great. After it was over I told her to come to Lincoln for a visit. We offered her a scholarship, she took it, and ended up becoming the National Player of the Year three years later.

I do not know why it had not occurred to me earlier, but it gets pitch black on the plains at night. When we went to leave Cambridge, I could not believe how dark it was. Typically at an airport the runway is all lit up. Out there you have the tiny headlight on the nose of the plane lighting your way and that's it. But we had an uneventful flight back to Lincoln and Todd and I became semi-regular flying partners after that.

Once, after a trip for a speaking engagement following the 2008 season, Todd recommended I get my pilot's license. He was happy to fly me when he could, but he thought the training would be good for me. He was also buying a small plane at the time and told me I could buy a share and use it to train and then fly it myself if I wanted to.

It was the right suggestion at the right time. I had been looking for ways to become a better coach and thought I needed to get out of my comfort zone a little bit, whether that was learning to play guitar or learning to fly. Flying a plane was a completely new challenge. It provided me the opportunity to occasionally get my mind off coaching by being coached by somebody else. Ultimately I wanted to learn how *I* wanted to be coached.

I got set up with a great instructor named Clay Barnes. Clay attended Lincoln Southeast High School, where he played football with Alex

Gordon, an eventual three-time MLB All-Star with the Kansas City Royals, and Barrett Ruud, a linebacker who played eight seasons in the NFL. Clay was a pretty good athlete himself, and played as a kicker on the Doane College football team. So we had some common ground in athletics. At the time I started training with him, Clay was working his way up as a pilot. In 2016 he was hired by Southwest Airlines, achieving his career dream.

My training started with ground school and everything was going fine. The first day we took a plane up, Clay let me take control of the plane, and we had no problems. It was a pretty magical feeling, actually.

About two weeks into our training, Clay told me that the day's lesson would be on crosswind landings. "Okay, great," I said, not fully knowing what was in store.

A crosswind landing is the way to land a plane, big or small, when dealing with a wind that blows perpendicular to the runway's centerline. If you have a north-south runway but an east-west wind, you have to turn the plane into the wind or else get blown off the runway. Essentially you must fly the plane sideways, which does not come naturally. Crosswind landings are a point of pride among pilots.

We start out doing practice runs at the Lincoln Airport. We didn't land, but stayed about 100 feet above the runway just to get used to flying the plane sideways. After doing that for a while, Clay told me to head to the Seward Airport about 15 miles west of Lincoln. This was in February. We got out there and I looked down at the tiny runway and it was covered in ice.

"We're landing on that?"

"Oh, yeah."

We came down for the first try and I could not keep the plane sideways long enough, so we pulled up and did a go-around. It was the first of many that day. I was ready to give up, but Clay told me we were not leaving until we got one right. Two hours later I finally did get the plane down in what had become sort of my own personal trash can drill.

As we flew back to Lincoln my hands were shaking so much that Clay had to land the plane. I got out and said, "I don't think I can do this."

Clay was there with encouragement. "You've just got to work through this," he said. "This is the toughest part."

What makes crosswind landings so tough is that they go against all of your instincts. You feel like if you land your plane sideways you will slide right off the runway, when in actuality that is what this type of landing is designed to prevent. I think most pilots are terrified the first time they attempt it, but Clay's mantra when we would practice these landings was to "trust your training."

I knew the moment he said it that I had just added something to my coaching repertoire. It is a great lesson for sports. Sometimes in athletics there are things we think we see and things we think will happen. There are times when the play or assignment will seem counterintuitive. But players must trust their training in such moments. The player that starts getting caught up in what they see or, worse, the player that starts guessing, is the player that gets beat.

Eventually I became comfortable enough with my crosswind landings that it was time for my first solo flight, which was only slightly less terrifying. I made my first trip to Hebron, a small town about sixty miles southwest of Lincoln. I had to navigate my own way to get there, using just the instruments and dead reckoning. My flight plan called for me to land, do a touch-and-go, and then fly back to Lincoln.

The flight went off without a hitch and on the way back I was finally able to just sort of marvel at how amazing it is to be up there all by yourself. Once you see the world from the air, you will see the world differently forever.

Eventually I got my license and was able to start flying myself for nearby recruiting visits to Denver, Kansas City, and Minneapolis. Tom Osborne was the athletic director at that point and I went to ask him if I could get reimbursed for the trips the way I would if I were driving. I was happy to take just the car mileage, but I wanted to get the flight hours. Eventually I put in around 250 hours.

Only then did Osborne tell me that he too had gotten his pilot's license while he was coaching. He told me had nearly 1,000 hours in the cockpit. I asked him why he had decided to do it and he told me about a time he was being flown to Wichita, Kansas, for an awards banquet. They were flying straight into a thunderstorm and he decided then that if he was going to take flights like that he needed to know how to land the plane himself in case anything went wrong.

Sure enough, whenever I landed at a small-town airport in Nebraska, I would ask some of the old-timers hanging around, crop dusters a lot of the time, if they ever remembered Osborne coming through. They almost always said they did and had the flight logs to prove it.

Maybe my most memorable flight was when I flew Wendy and Lauren to Manhattan, Kansas. Lauren was taking a recruiting visit to Kansas State and the plan was that she and Wendy would go check out the campus and facilities while I just stayed at the airport. I brought along a pilot with us just to be safe, and for most of the flight it was a perfect day. As we began our approach, however, the wind picked up and things started to get bumpy. Landing in Manhattan was going to require a crosswind landing.

I was psyched up to show what I could do. I trusted my training, cranked the plane sideways, and nailed the landing. But the entire time I could feel Wendy bracing herself against the back of my seat. She pulled me aside once we were out of the plane and made her feelings known. "Why were you flying the plane sideways?" she asked. "Are you sure you know how to fly?"

That is what a crosswind landing feels like to the person who has never experienced one before. It is so far outside what someone expects that you cannot help but think something is wrong. The trip produced two results: Lauren said no to Kansas State and Wendy never flew with me again.

Overall, learning to flying was a transformative experience for me and I got exactly what I wanted and needed out of it. Being up there and placing all of my trust in Clay, while Clay was up there placing a great deal of trust in me, was really intense, terrifying, and stressful. But I enjoyed the training. It allowed me to pay attention to how I was being coached.

That in turn changed how I coached. I realized I needed to change as a coach and, most important, that I *could* change. I learned that there were other ways to coach beyond just coaching like a football coach, with super intensity all the time.

I kept Clay's mantra—"Trust your training"—in my coaching notebook for a long time after that, and it became one of our most consistent messages at Nebraska in the years to come. In fact, it was so important that it was one of the messages written on our whiteboard before we headed out to face Texas for the national title match in 2015.

In this world it is hard to trust. And though it is one of the hardest things to build, the longer I coach the more I think it is one of the defining characteristics of any successful team. We are always talking about trust. Trust your training. Trust your coaches. Trust your game plan. Trust your teammates. Most important, trust yourself.

It is an easy thing to preach but a tough thing to teach. When your team does not have trust, others notice. I still remember playing Texas in the regional final in Lincoln in 2013. The Longhorns were the top-ranked team in the country, while we were ranked No. 9. That 2013 team was a strange mix of players. Our top hitter, Kelsey Robinson, and setter Mary Pollmiller were both transfers from the University of Tennessee, playing in their first season at Nebraska. Kadie Rolfzen and Amber Rolfzen were freshmen who had come to Nebraska with perhaps the most hype surrounding them of any in-state prospects ever. Justine Wong-Orantes, a setter in high school, was our true freshman libero.

Texas was rolling us out of our own gym, winning the first two sets 25–19 and 25–22. Things were chaotic, but we showed some fight in the third set, building a 17–15 lead. Texas reeled off 3 straight points after that, with the last coming on a serve that Kelsey Robinson let go as it was headed long. Amber Rolfzen did not get out of the way, however, and the ball hit her to give a point to Texas. I took Amber out at that point and tried to give her some coaching, but she stared off into the distance and wouldn't make eye contact with me. Karch Kiraly, working the ESPN telecast, noted something very important. "If you're Texas, you've got to look at the body language of Nebraska," he said. "They are a beaten team here. They're not looking each other in the eye. They're not carrying each other with any kind of strength or shoulders up."

Karch has seen, played, and coached a lot of volleyball. What he was noticing was the thing you never want to be apparent with one of your teams, but he was right. Our body language was one of defeat. You could see that our players were pulling into themselves, focusing on what they needed to do rather than giving of themselves and playing for each other.

We delayed elimination for a few more points. A kill from Kelsey made it 22–22, and even Karch thought we might be showing some life. "That is the first time I've seen all the Huskers look each other in the eye the whole set, maybe most of the match," he said following the point.

It was too little, too late, however. We did not have the trust necessary to win that game. Texas closed out the third set with a 3–1 run and our season was over.

The trust was not there at the end of the 2014 season, either. After knocking off third-ranked Washington on its home floor in the Seattle regional semifinal, we were set to face a BYU team that was not one of the sixteen national seeds in the tournament. To lose that match would have been a mild upset. To get swept was nearly unthinkable. But that is exactly what happened. We lost the serve-and-pass battle in a big way, and that led to big trouble against the best blocking team in the country. When our passes were not on the mark you could sense the trust start to break down.

Headed into the 2015 season we realized that we had to do something about the trust issue. We had been using "Trust your training" as a mantra for a couple of seasons by that point, and we felt like we needed to up the intensity even more. As we sat down in January to plan out the season we asked ourselves as coaches how we could make the trust issue stronger than ever. That is when we came up with what we called "ultimate trust."

We introduced the concept of ultimate trust to our players and asked them to each find a photo of what ultimate trust looks like. We got some photos of trust falls and we got some photos of skydivers with their parachutes. The one that hit the mark the hardest was a photo of two dogs, one with the other dog's leash in its mouth. It was not until you looked closer that you could tell that the dog being led was blind. Everyone loves dogs, so it was not a total surprise that that was the photo that stuck. It became a prized visual representation of what we were after that season.

Achieving that level of ultimate trust, however, was still a process. We did not have it early in the season, particularly during the weekend we lost to both Minnesota and Wisconsin. You could tell from our huddles after points. It was not a tight huddle. The players would go in like they always do, but they were not fully there, whether celebrating a point won or regrouping after a point lost. It was a token gathering, really.

Trust can reveal itself in interesting, even accidental, ways. A few years prior to that 2015 season, Terry Pettit called me up and asked me why I sat on the bench all the time during matches. His argument was that it did not look like I was engaged in the match.

My rebuttal was that Russ Rose, the coach at Penn State, never left the bench and he had seven national titles. But I decided to try being more active on the sideline.

I did that for a few seasons, but as we headed into the 2015 NCAA Tournament I had a hurt back. It was more comfortable for me to sit down. So I sat and a funny thing happened. Following a tough early match when the team had to work itself out of some trouble, our setter mentioned in the postgame interviews that the fact that I stayed seated indicated how much I trusted the team to work through it.

It was totally a matter of chance that I was sitting down for that match, but if that is what it took for the team to see the ultimate trust on my end, I was more than happy to let it work. If they thought I was sitting down because I knew they had it wired and that gave them tremendous confidence, ownership, and trust in what they were doing, maybe I should have been sitting down anyway.

It really was not until our final match against Texas that season that I knew we had met our goal of "ultimate trust" across the board. Late in the match against the Longhorns, Amber Rolfzen got a kill on the slide and our team had maybe its tightest postpoint huddle of the season. It was the opposite of what Karch noticed in 2013. This huddle was as tight as could be. The players were not putting their hands on each other's backs in a token display; they were arm in arm and as close as could be. This huddle was a reflection of their belief in each other. It was a reflection of how far that group had come, how close the big dream felt to becoming a reality, and how confident the players were that they were ready to achieve it. Few people probably even noticed it, but it was the purest display of ultimate trust I had ever seen.

A few years ago, after reading Pete Carroll's book, *Win Forever*, I decided to boil my coaching philosophy down to twenty-five words or less. I ended up at twenty-eight, which maybe should not come as a surprise, given my proclivity for themes that have developed over the years. I ended up with this:

> Dream big. Set big goals and work to see it, believe it, and achieve it. Compete every day to be the best. Develop ultimate trust in our team.

There is great value in trying to reduce your leadership philosophy down to its most basic elements. Trying to be succinct is how you learn what is really at the core of what you believe. Those are the words you can and should lean on when you are unsure about what you are doing. Those days of question come for any coach. Those days will derail you if you let them. But you should never lose sight of the beliefs that lie at the heart of what you do. Often you will find the real reason you signed up for a position of leadership: to improve the lives of others. Giving what you have so that others may receive it is one of the noblest pursuits there is, no matter the endeavor. The job will challenge that idea time and time again, but it is important to continue to give.

It is also okay if those core beliefs change over the course of a career. If anything, my life as a coach is defined by being open to new ideas, by being willing to change, by being receptive to the insights of others, and by being able to treat each new season, each new team, as a journey that is different from ones that came before it.

The popular view of the winning coach is that of a taskmaster, the person with all the ideas and the proven system. I think that is the wrong point of view. If you are leading for the right reasons, your core beliefs will simply be the building blocks for new ways of thinking about your sport. They will be the foundation for how you approach teaching, but only that—the foundation. Successful coaching is really about team building and, once you have laid the foundation, the team you build on top of it can take many forms. It has to, because no matter how many players have or will come in and out of your program, no matter how many big games you have won or lost, each team and each player has different needs. The coach that best understands this and is willing to work as hard as he or she did on day one is the coach best prepared to succeed.

If you go back to that twenty-eight-word philosophy, what does it actually say? It says we will not compromise when it comes to goal-setting. It says we will not shy away from working toward those goals. It says we are confident enough to both put in the work and make a point to share our goals with others, making them tangible beyond the confines of our program. It says that we recognize that achieving those goals requires a daily commitment, spurred by a forward-thinking and comprehensive knowledge of today's athlete, a commitment that few are actually willing to make. It says that nothing matters more than the trust the entire team has for one another.

You can win this way. You can improve and you can refine. But, more than that, you can build incredible teams and incredible individuals. It is how we have done it at Nebraska.

Epilogue

I checked a big item off my coaching bucket list before I had even coached my first game as the head coach at Nebraska. Before the 2000 season started in the fall, we took our team to China. We knew it would be a valuable team-building experience. Taking a bunch of players, many of them from small towns in and around Nebraska, and showing them just how big and beautiful the world is gets to my philosophy of training complete athletes: exposing them to things beyond the volleyball court so they are ready to go off into life, whether that life includes volleyball or not, with some experiences under their belts.

One of the biggest reasons for that trip was that nobody had ever taken a college volleyball team to China before. A few years earlier the Wisconsin team I coached became the first team to go to Russia. Going to China, given the political climate and diplomatic relations at the time, was probably even a bigger logistical challenge, which, from my point of view, made it even more worth doing.

Before we left for China I went to speak to the Husker Beef Club, a collection of cattlemen and ranchers in Nebraska who donate to the athletic department, many times in the form of a side of beef. I gave my talk, which included news of our China trip, and after it was over one of the boosters came up to me and said it was great that we were going but that the powerful football program with its decades-long sellout streak and all the revenue it generated was the reason we were able to make the trip. At that point in time he was not wrong. At most schools football and men's basketball, the so-called revenue sports, generate the vast majority of the money needed to fund the other sports that a college can offer. I decided that day, however, that this was not going to be the case for Nebraska volleyball. I set a goal of making volleyball a revenue-producing sport. Eventually we needed to pay our own way so no one could ever say to me again that "football pays for all of this."

Twelve years later the athletic department announced the construction of Pinnacle Bank Arena, a new facility in downtown Lincoln that was going to be the home of men's and women's basketball. That meant the Bob Devaney Sports Center was available and everybody started doing the math. I got calls from reporters the day of the announcement, asking if volleyball was going to move to the Devaney Center full time.

Everyone in our program loved the Coliseum. It was sold out every night. The crowd was right on top of you, which offered a real home-court advantage. We had won nearly 94 percent of our matches at the Coliseum since the founding of the program in 1975. There was a ton of history in that building. It was our volleyball version of Kansas's Allen Fieldhouse or Duke's Cameron Indoor Stadium. I was in no hurry to leave, whether the Devaney Center was available or not.

"Why would we go there?" I asked one of the reporters who had called. "If it's not good enough for basketball, it's not good enough for volleyball." When my comments ran in the newspaper the next day, I got a call from Tom Osborne. "Get to the office right now," he told me over the phone. Some of the people who work in the Athletic Department later told me they had never seen Osborne as mad as he was that morning. I showed up at his office and he did not mince any words.

"What are you doing?" he asked me.

"Coach," I said, "that's how I really feel. Why would we move there if it's no longer good enough for basketball?"

Osborne asked what he could do to make it better. Right then and there I wrote a list of seven things that needed to happen to turn the Devaney Center into a volleyball facility.

"We'll make it happen," Osborne said. "If we do, you'll go?"

"We'll go."

Osborne delivered on those promises and in 2013 we played our first season in a totally revamped Devaney Center. We were able to double our capacity from 4,000 at the Coliseum to more than 8,000 at the new arena. With that extra ticket revenue, the volleyball program turned a profit for the first time and I was able to check off another item on my coaching bucket list.

Having a list like that—I call mine the Dream Big Bucket List—is important for anyone who wishes to be successful. Fill it with the biggest ideas you can imagine, look at it often, and then begin putting in the work necessary to start checking items off the list. I feel incredibly fortunate to have checked off many items on my list in my years coaching volleyball.

Nebraska football has the longest-standing stadium sellout streak in the country. Memorial Stadium has been sold out for every game since November 3, 1962. Why couldn't we start our own sellout streak? Thanks to the undying loyalty of Husker fans we did accomplished that 2001 and it is still going, despite doubling our seating capacity in 2013. At the end of the 2016 season we had played in front of a sellout crowd for 219 consecutive matches. Moving to the Devaney Center also allowed us to become the first college volleyball program to sell standing-room-only tickets and become the first program with a Taraflex floor, the same court used in the Olympics.

Nebraska was also the first college volleyball program to erect a bronze statue. Terry Pettit, a native of the Chicago area, saw that the Chicago Bulls put up a statue of Michael Jordan in the early 1990s outside of the United Center and wanted to do the same for the Coliseum. Pettit found a sculptor, Nebraska-native George Lundeen, and commissioned a bronze sculpture that was placed at the entrance to the Coliseum. To pay for it Pettit sold one hundred miniatures of the statues to some of Nebraska volleyball's top boosters. When it came time to move to the Devaney Center, I made sure that a special spot was built for that sculpture, which allowed us to take a little of the Coliseum with us.

Nebraska is not the first place people think of when they think of the beach. In fact, it may be one of the last. But we were not going to let that stop us from starting a beach volleyball program. We built an indoor sand court, another first for a college program, and started the first beach volleyball program in the Midwest in 2013.

Flying with the Blue Angels was not just a career-long dream of mine; it was also a lifelong dream. As a kid those Top Gun–style pilots flew over my head every day, so that dream embedded itself in my head at a very young age. After being told I was too tall to fly the jets myself, I finally got to go up in a fighter jet in 2006. The Blue Angels were in Lincoln for the annual airshow, but it was during our season so they offered the baseball coach, Mike Anderson, the opportunity to go up with them. He had had back surgery in the off-season so he couldn't pass the physical to do it. I got a call on Tuesday and they asked if I wanted to go up the following day. We were scheduled to face Iowa State that night in Lincoln, but there was no way I was missing my chance. I called Dr. Lonnie Albers, the director of athletic medicine at Nebraska, asked him to give me a physical that morning, and got to live out my dream of flying with the Blue Angels. I am pretty certain I am the only volleyball coach to have flown with the Blue Angels. I am totally certain I am the only coach to have ever been inside both an F/A-18 Hornet and a nuclear submarine, something I checked off the list when I spent a night aboard the USS *Nebraska*.

Memorable moments such as those do not just make me proud of what we have accomplished at Nebraska. I think they are a big part of why we have had success. By dreaming big and setting the goals to match those dreams, we have asked more of ourselves than many thought we could give. There is only one place to go from there—to dream bigger.

We headed to the locker room of the Devaney Center on December 9, 2016, with our season hanging in the balance and it was barely even noon. It had been a magical but grueling season up to that point. Trying to defend a national championship always is, but the Big 10 was as strong as it had ever been in 2016.

We opened the season as the preseason No. 1 team in the country and were ranked at the top of twelve of the sixteen polls in 2016. Minnesota and Wisconsin each spent all but one week ranked in the top five. Penn State was ranked each week and finished tenth in the final poll. Michigan, Ohio State, and Michigan State all finished ranked as well. Purdue and Illinois spent about half of the 2016 season in the top twenty-five. That is what we played against night in and night out. It was a grind every night, but we finished 18-2 in Big 10 play and locked up the conference title on the last night of the regular season with a win over Michigan.

Winning the Big Ten was one of our top goals in 2016. Our senior class—Kadie Rolfzen, Amber Rolfzen, and Justine Wong-Orantes—had won a national title, but they had yet to win a conference title. I had said all season long that winning the Big Ten was tougher than winning the NCAA Tournament. Winning the Big 10 requires two months of excellence over twenty matches. The tournament requires 6 wins in a row. There was no comparison between the two, but we had our sights set on doing both and becoming the first team at Nebraska to defend its national title.

We earned the top overall seed in the tournament, which, under a new tournament format, gave us the edge of hosting our first four matches at the Devaney Center. The draw did us no favors, however. Washington, the No. 7 national seed, was in the Lincoln bracket, as was No. 16 Penn State. Going back to 2005, Washington, Nebraska, or Penn State had won nine of the previous eleven national titles. We went from the grind of the Big 10 and into the grind of a tough tournament bracket almost overnight.

After sweeping New Hampshire and TCU in the first two rounds, everyone got the Penn State–Nebraska matchup they were pointing to as a possibility when the bracket was revealed. We had already beaten the Nittany Lions twice in 2016, gutting out a 5-set win at their place in early November and sweeping them in Lincoln two weeks later. Those previous wins gave me little peace of mind. I knew deep down how good Penn State was. I knew how well they could play and our players did too. It was a pressure-packed week.

ESPNU made the decision to televise all the regional semifinals for the first time in the network's history. It was great for the sport of volleyball, but it meant one match had to start at 11:00 a.m., and that match was ours. We adjusted our typical game preparation based on some of our sleep and peak-performance data and got ready to try and beat Penn State for the third time in 2016.

Right out of the gate Penn State head coach Russ Rose sent his team out to the court in a 6-2, something the Nittany Lions had not run all year. It was a savvy move as it changed the matchups and, after fourteen ties and four lead changes, Penn State was two points better in the first set, winning 25-23.

That opening-set loss seemed to give us a spark in set 2, as we jumped out to a 7-2 lead. Penn State battled back from there, then we edged back in front at 22-19, but the Nittany Lions closed the set on a 6-1 run and were again just two points better.

We were the No. 1 seed and down 2 sets on our home floor, but the locker room at the break was remarkably calm. I already knew that calm and confident was going to be my approach when I spoke to the team, but that confidence only grew when I got to the locker room and saw that the team, while a little shocked, was displaying the same calm. I made two cases to the team.

One, I told them we were going to change our rotation. We switched to rotation five because I wanted to get one of our best servers that season the first serve in the third game. What I really wanted to do, however, was get our sophomore outside hitter more time in the front row. She had shown a knack for showing up in big matches, but I did not tell our team that. Sometimes some things are best left unsaid. We do not change our rotation very often, but I thought that a different lineup, similar to the switch Penn State had made by going to a 6-2 at the start of the match, would give us some hope. It was my way of saying to the players that I thought I had an answer, that I had thought things through.

Two, I told the team we could do this. I looked right at Dani Busboom Kelly and told our players about the time Dani's team was down 2-0 to Minnesota in the regional final in Florida in 2006. "We can come back and do this," I told them. "You've got to be ready to grind hard for three games."

We went back out for the third set and played well early, building a 9–3 lead and forcing a Penn State time-out. We held a 6-point margin all the way to 16–10, but the Nittany Lions started to claw their way back from there. I called a time-out at 16–14. Coach Rose called his second time-out when we took a 22–19 lead. His time-out spurred a 5–0 run for Penn State and we were down to our last point.

The Devaney Center was on edge, but even at that point I never thought we were going to lose the match. In 2006, when we fell behind 2–0 to Minnesota, I thought the match was over and we had blown a remarkable season, but that thought never crossed my mind this time. We went into that match knowing it was going to be tough and, down 24–22 while facing a 2–0 deficit, things were as tough as they could possibly get. But I never thought we were going to lose.

Amber Rolfzen got a kill to make it 24–23, then she combined on a block with the setter to make it 24–24. The sophomore outside hitter took it from there, recording back-to-back kills to win the third set and keep us alive. Part of my confidence in that match came from playing at home. I knew that if we could turn things around and win a set, the Devaney Center crowd would become an advantage and it did. We won the fourth set 25–19 and then controlled the fifth set, winning 15–6. Our season was saved.

I had a feeling that, having cleared the Penn State hurdle, we would play pretty free and loose after that. One of our themes for 2016 was "Good to great to unstoppable." We felt unstoppable the next night. We made quick work of Washington, winning 25–16, 25–10, 25–21, and punched our ticket to Columbus, Ohio, achieving another goal we had been seeing, sharing, and wearing all year long, with our references to 1492. Texas, the team we had beaten in Omaha for the 2015 title, awaited us in the national semifinal.

That is where our season ended. The Longhorns swept us, becoming the only team to sweep us that season. I have learned over the years that it is hardest to play a team with nothing to lose. That was Texas. We had swept them earlier in the season. We swept them to win the 2015 national title. The Longhorns were plenty good, but they had the "Let's go knock these guys off" bounce in their step that is always hard to match if you do not match it right away. We did not.

That loss remains a mystery to me. I felt great in the week leading up to the game. We had a great a week of practice and the players were loose and confident. When the lights went on and we saw the look in Texas's eyes, however, we tightened up.

After the match I told the reporters that I would not have changed one thing about how we prepared for that match. I am pretty honest when it comes to those things. In 2001, when we lost to Stanford in the championship match, I knew why we had lost. In 2007, during our second attempt at defending a title, I could feel us coming apart at the seams. Those losses were black and white. I could see them coming. I knew what our weaknesses were and did not have a good feeling in my gut heading into those matches.

The Texas match? A few weeks after the season, that one still remained a shocker. It was eating at me, but not in the way a loss like that would have earlier in my career. I knew by then that it did not change anything about 2016. It did not change how good of a coach I was. It did not diminish any of the individual and team breakthroughs that were made leading up to that match. It did not change the effort anyone in the program had put toward making our biggest dreams come true.

Our theme for 2016 was Dreaming Bigger, and there is no question we did that. It just did not work out. That's sports. It's what makes them worth playing and worth following. It's what makes them interesting and one of the best metaphors for life itself. It is what makes them worthy of a lifetime of devotion, and I am but one of many who have been fortunate enough to give my life to the growth we find through the games we play.

It was not obvious to me why or how we lost to Texas in 2016, but I can tell you this: I could not wait to get back to the office, back to practice, back with my team, to begin the work again. That is the true reward of being a coach: every season is like a lifetime lived anew.